THE FAMILY HISTORY PROJECT

great great stories from the nation's family tree

the national archives

First published in association with The History Channel in 2004 by

The National Archives
Kew, Richmond, Surrey
TW9 4DU, UK

www.nationalarchives.gov.uk/

The National Archives (TNA) was formed when the Public Record Office (PRO) and Historical Manuscripts Commission (HMC) combined in April 2003.

The History Channel
Grant Way
Isleworth, Middlesex
TW7 5QD, UK

A catalogue record for this book is available from the British Library.

ISBN 1 903365 75 9

Pages designed and typeset by Carnegie Publishing, Lancaster, Lancashire

Printed in the UK by Cromwell Press, Trowbridge, Wiltshire

Contents

The stories in this book have been edited for best presentation, but otherwise are as entered into The Family History Project. Although The History Channel and The National Archives have made every effort to check the accuracy of the stories, they cannot be held responsible for any errors that remain.

Introduction

If you have picked up this book, then you probably have at least a passing interest in one of the most popular pastimes in Britain today – genealogy, or family history as it is more commonly known. Every day, legions of researchers head into county and national archives. They scour the pages of historic documents for clues concerning distant relatives that, up till now, have been lost in the mists of time. Perhaps you are already part of this archival army, and have spent many happy (or frustrating) hours searching for information to add to your family tree.

On the other hand, you may be a complete beginner to family history. It is possible that you have heard friends talk about their quest for long-forgotten ancestors but have never considered the possibility of doing this yourself. The stories showcased in this book are some of the more remarkable entries submitted to The Family History Project, an initiative run by The History Channel to encourage people to start looking into their families' past. Many of the contributors started from scratch, and the fruits of their labours should inspire you to set off on your own detective trail; like them, you never know what you will uncover!

As a historian and research genealogist, I have had the pleasure and privilege to act as both project consultant and one of the judges, along with Elaine Collins (*Ancestors* magazine), Dan Finch (The History Channel), Maggie Loughran (Federation of Family History Societies), Geoff Metzger (The History Channel), Martin Morgan (The History Channel), William Spencer (The National Archives) and Garrick Webster (*Your Family Tree* magazine). Therefore I feel that I should start with a confession: I have not researched my own family tree. This sorry state of affairs was not brought about by a lack of desire but because my uncles and great-uncles have already made a thorough investigation over the years. So I know that my mother's family originates from eighteenth-century French Huguenot immigrants, and that on my father's side I have roots in Lancashire. Yet although I now spend much of my time untangling other people's family histories, I still find great excitement in successfully tracking down an elusive individual via official certificates, census returns, wills, property records and a wide variety of other documents that partially record their life and times.

Family history as a research discipline

One of the joys of genealogy is that there is always something else to discover. Furthermore, the path you will follow when tracking your ancestors back in time is likely to be unique. This means that family historians quickly develop a wide range of research skills.

On a practical level, you will need patience and a dogged determination. If you want to find a relative who lived in one of Britain's growing cities in the mid-nineteenth century, it may simply be a case of working through endless reels of microfilmed census returns. Time is therefore an important consideration, as is cost; and you may need to devote more resources if you are searching for an ancestor with a common name, such as Smith or Jones. For example, if you have a rough date of birth for someone, you can check the birth registration indexes and compile a list of people born with the same name in the area in which you think they lived, but to ensure you get the right one, you may need to order all these certificates, bearing in mind that each costs at least £7.

The further back in time you work, the more you have to look at several sources in combination, particularly at a local level. While this can be a daunting prospect at first, using more than one type of document offers a unique opportunity to do more than simply add new generations to your family tree. Obviously it is important to compile an accurate a family tree; but there could come a time when you are simply collecting names without thinking about who these people were and what their lives were like. If your family tree can be compared to a skeleton, the fun part of your research should be to put the flesh back on the bones by providing context.

As you will see, some of the more interesting stories in the book are those from contributors who have placed them within the political, social and economic climate of the day.

It is important to use occupation and residency data from census returns and certificates to start other lines of work, sometimes not directly linked to a quest to find another ancestor. What was the main source of employment in the town? What was their house like? Were they workers or employers? What was happening at the time in the country at large? How did this affect the local area? These are some of the questions that you should consider every time you add a new line to your family tree.

The importance of family history today

So aside from the personal thrill of tracking down an elusive ancestor or confirming a family legend, why are people curious about their past? Many column inches have been devoted to theories about the phenomenon, and there is no single satisfactory reason. I believe that an important part of the yearning to trace our roots lies in the nature of today's society. Information technology has revolutionised the way in which we communicate with one another, while our busy lives are often spent many miles from where we grew up. We may think nothing of emailing people half way around the world, yet spend less time each year with our extended families. Britain has a rich oral history, but in the modern age we are in real danger of losing the experiences and memories of previous generations.

At the start of the twentieth century, the majority of people lived in the vicinity of their immediate family, and story-telling at regular gatherings would ensure family legend and folklore would be passed down from generation to generation. The two world wars, greater internal migration and the reliance on first radio and then television for entertainment have changed this way of life forever. It is a sad irony that this same technology offers, for perhaps the first time in

Dan Finch of The History Channel presents Christine Prytherch with her prize, on the Winners' Day at the National Archives on 8 April 2004

history, an entire generation the opportunity to record its thoughts, feelings and experiences for posterity, yet we are in danger of letting this vital information slip through our fingers.

In Britain, we are blessed with a rich history but historians have tended to chronicle major events and the people who defined our nation's development. The everyday folk who lived through these momentous events have tended to get overlooked in the textbooks – until now. Family history allows you to bring your ancestors back to life; by telling their stories you are giving a voice to Britain's forgotten sections of society.

The Family History Project

Following on from recent 'personal heritage' projects, such as A Small Piece of History, The History Channel has recognised the urgent need to reconcile modern technological advances with the capture and preservation of personal history. Consequently, The Family History Project was created to encourage people to talk to their older relatives, record these stories and experiences, look for family heirlooms or clues, and use this evidence to start wider research into the origins of their family. A website was created (www.thefamilyhistoryproject.co.uk) to help newcomers to the field, which offered advice ranging from how to organise data into a family tree to practical tips when tackling the most important primary sources – certificates, census and parish registers.

One of the most exciting elements of the project was the 'call to arms' in the form of a competition to find the most interesting stories about our ancestors. A team of genealogists, including Paul Blake and Maggie Loughran from the Federation of Family History Societies, attended various events around the UK to promote the project. The recent proliferation of history programmes on television has clearly generated interest in the subject, but although people were incredibly enthusiastic about the thought of 'doing' history themselves, it was clear that the greatest obstacle for beginners was a lack of confidence in how and where to start the research. Once they had been given the basics – talk to relatives, look for family documents, write it down and compile a tree – most were fired up and eager to tackle primary sources in archives.

It is no exaggeration to say that we were overwhelmed by the response to the competition – more than 3,500 entrants submitted their stories, ranging in experience from the absolute beginner to the seasoned researcher of many years. The quality and range of stories was breathtaking, and I hope you enjoy the selection published here as much as we did in choosing them. The stories have been grouped into broad themes and categories, and will hopefully spur you on to find out more about your past.

Nick Barratt

The Stories

A New Life

Family history can be a difficult enough pursuit at the best of times, but, if our ancestors moved around the world, the task of the researcher is even more difficult. The stories in this section are remarkable in their own right, but they become even more astonishing when you bear in mind the research that was required to verify them.

A particularly good example of this is Christine Prytherch's search for her natural parents, having learned at the age of 17 that she was adopted. Even under normal circumstances, adoption can be a tricky subject to research, but given the obstacles she came up against, her search was made even more difficult.

The stories printed here reflect contrasting experiences of people who lived during the heyday of the British Empire. One tale takes us to Australia, where convicts were transported to serve terms in prison colonies. There are accounts of missionaries who left British shores to work voluntarily overseas. Not everyone came back, as you will discover.

Equally, Britain has been seen as a place of refuge over the centuries, and we have included the tale of a French Communard who fled from Paris when the French army regained control of the capital in 1871. Another story features a man who moved across three continents – quite a feat for the time, and even more of a challenge for his descendants to research!

Research Tips

Migrant ancestors can be difficult to track down, and many essential resources for your research are likely to be deposited outside Britain. Nevertheless, there are some lines of research you can pursue here before considering contacting an overseas archive. For example, transportation records – and the trial proceedings that resulted in transportation – can be found at the National Archives. You will also find correspondence and administration material relating to the government and daily life in Britain's former colonies. Relations with foreign powers were conducted through the Foreign Office, and the movements and activities of British nationals abroad can be traced through their records.

The British in India can be investigated at the British Library, where the archives of the East India Company and subsequent British administration are located in the Oriental and India Office Library. Several colleges within the University of London have substantial manuscript archives, for example the School of Oriental and African Studies, while there are numerous museums and institutions devoted to the study of Empire and Commonwealth.

For people moving to Britain, standard genealogical sources are of some use, such as census returns, but you might want to consider naturalisation and residency applications. Many immigrant communities established their own places of worship, which can be researched at local archives and specialist institutions.

I discovered who I really was

Having had a normal childhood, I was devastated to discover at 17 that I was adopted. Suspicions arose when I needed a passport for a proposed visit to Germany. I had longed for years to learn German and visit the country. Despite strong opposition from my parents, I arranged an exchange with a German girl. My parents were not willing to tell me anything and it was only months after my trip that they told me I was adopted and had been born in Germany. No other information was given to me, but I determined that one day I would find out where I had come from.

In the arms of Martha Weiss, the midwife who delivered me

4

My German birth
certificate of 1937

At 50, I started searching and eventually discovered I had indeed been born in Germany in 1937, after Hitler had risen to power and begun to persecute the Jews. As my mother was an unmarried Jewess and my father a Nazi, the situation was not good and she brought me back to England, where I was later adopted.

My research took me back to Germany where I met the midwife who had delivered me 50 years earlier! She gave me photos, taken by my mother, of me newborn in her arms. These photos had survived the terrible bombing that Freiburg suffered when most of the town was destroyed. Returning to England, I met two of my mother's sisters and a cousin. My mother had died five years earlier, but this did not matter. I had discovered, at last, who I really was!

Christine Prytherch

Members of the Muskogee tribe

My family origins have always been a mystery to me. I started to investigate them as I have dark skin, inherited from my father, but as he was adopted we never knew our origins. My father's adoption papers revealed that his birth father was an American Indian GI called Freeman Marshall.

Freeman Marshall

After extensive research I tracked Freeman's last known address to Coweta, Oklahoma. Following a notice I posted on the town's website I received an email from Freeman's cousin from South Carolina who had not seen him in nearly 50 years. He put me in touch with my grandfather's relations who were ecstatic to discover their new family. Within days I began to receive emails from long-lost cousins across America.

In July 2000 I travelled to Oklahoma. My grandfather was then 91 years old and had developed Alzheimer's, but confirmed my grandmother's name, and I was able to spend some wonderful moments with him, made all the more special by the fact that he died a few months later.

My introduction to American–Indian life was a whirlwind experience. My story appeared in the local paper; I visited the Indian church where I was related either by blood or clan to almost the entire congregation; and I met the chief and ate traditional food with the elder Indians at the tribal headquarters. As a result of my research my father is now the proud holder of an American passport and my father, brother and I are full members of the Muskogee tribe.

Lucy Grimster

The man who caught elephants

'To the Rev. D. Sanderson from his affectionate son, June 1878' – so reads the inscription on the title page of a book I inherited called *Thirteen Years Among the Wild Beasts of India.* The Rev. Daniel Sanderson, my paternal great-grandfather, was a Methodist missionary in India, from 1842 to 1867. 'His affectionate son' was George Perress Sanderson, the author of the book and my great-uncle.

G. P. Sanderson was born in India in 1848 and sent home for schooling to his father's family in Cockermouth, Cumbria. He was at the Wesley (Methodist) Kingswood School, Bath, from 1859 to 1863,

G. P. Sanderson (centre front), with Prince Albert behind on the left and the Maharajah of Mysore behind on the right

An illustration from
Thirteen Years Among the
Wild Beasts of India

returning to India, aged 16, in 1864. While employed by the
Government, he had time for hunting big game which included tigers,
elephants and bison.

G. P. Sanderson introduced a novel way of catching wild elephants
for subsequent taming and training in forestry work. Instead of
trapping elephants in pits, he tried driving herds into a 'keddah', a
fenced, ditched enclosure. This technique was a spectacular success
and in 1889 he organised a demonstration to entertain Prince Albert,
Duke of Clarence and Avondale, when he visited India. Prince Albert
was the eldest son of Edward, Prince of Wales, who later became
Edward VII.

In an article published by the Kipling Society in 1971, my father
provided convincing evidence that 'Petersen Sahib, the man who
caught all the elephants for the Government of India' in the Rudyard
Kipling's *Jungle Book* story, 'Toomai of the Elephants', was George
Perress Sanderson.

Theodore Tasker

An old Communard

My great-great-grandfather arrived in London, a refugee, in the summer of 1871. He had fled the slaughter of Bloody Week when the French Army regained control of Paris.

Zephirin Camelinat was born in Burgundy in 1840, and as a teenager he moved to Paris to become a bronze worker. He became a socialist, following the political philosopher Proudhon. By the late 1860s he was involved with the creation of the first International

Zephirin's funeral cortege in Paris, 1932. His hearse was followed by 120,000 people and the flags of over 100 nations lined the route. He was finally interred in Mailly La Ville, the little village in Burgundy where he was born. The tomb is still maintained by Les Amis de La Commune. He remains a potent symbol of international socialism and French nationalism.

Zephirin Camelinat in 1924, shortly after the founding of the French Communist Party

Working Men's Association. The Franco–Prussian War intervened, and Zephirin and his girlfriend Zoe were besieged in Paris with their two children, Jeanne and Eugene.

At the end of the war there was a popular rebellion against the harsh French government and Paris was seized by revolutionaries. Zephirin was elected to run the Paris Mint. The Commune lasted six weeks, and Zephirin fought right up to the end. When the last barricade fell, he was hidden by a local police chief. He shaved off his beard and went underground until he could board a ship for London.

Zephirin and Zoe lived in poverty in London. They had another child, Albert, but he died within a few months, soon followed by Zoe. Zephirin moved to Birmingham to work as a bronze worker. There he remarried and fathered another two daughters.

In 1880 the French declared an amnesty for the Communards and Zephirin returned to Paris. His children Jeanne and Eugene remained in Birmingham. Zephirin went on to become a founder of the French Communist Party and a well-respected politician until his death in 1932.

Nick Billingham

Fighting injustice in Kenya

This is a story of a remarkable man, my grandfather, Alibhai Mullah Jeevanjee.

From humble beginnings in the Indian sub-continent he travelled to Australia as a stowaway and later travelled to Kenya, East Africa. There, in the later part of the nineteenth century, he built a business empire stretching from Mombasa and Nairobi to Bombay and Karachi. He had a social and political impact that has not been equalled in that country.

Mr Jeevanjee was a member of the Indian Legislative Council, fighting for equal rights for all the people at a time when Kenya was a British colony. He took his fight to Whitehall, even though he was a man of little or no formal education. Mr Jeevanjee was a respected adversary of the white ruling classes in East Africa.

He travelled widely in Europe at a time when this was unheard of for someone of his ethnic origin. In Kenya, he founded the first English-language newspaper, which is still published, and made the construction of the railways possible.

Mr Jeevanjee, who owned large tracts of land in Nairobi, gave a three-acre site to the local authority as a gift. The park in the centre of the city still bears his name.

Mr Jeevanjee lost all his wealth and died in 1936 having lived modestly towards the end of his extraordinary life.

A great philanthropist and deeply religious man, he used his wealth and power to fight injustice wherever he encountered it. His legacy and all he believed in still lives on.

Aftab Jeevanjee

The story of a hero's trials

By CIUGU MWAGIRU

An eloquent, tireless fighter for justice who built Nairobi from scratch, made a fortune and lost it

When, in June 1991, the land grabbing brigade trained its sights on Nairobi's Jeevanjee Gardens, the local media were quick to blow the whistle, trig-off a public furore the likes of which had been known in Kenya.

Alibhai Mulla Jeevanjee, a rotund spic and span after whom the gardens are named and who ... on our shores in 1890, probably had the greatest impact on Kenya's social, political economic history during the nearly five decades that he spent in the country before his death a heart attack in 1936. What is more, the man ... dited with having almost single-handedly ... p the original Nairobi.

... years referred to as ''The Grand Old Man of ... '', a title that was only much later bestowed ... late President Jomo Kenyatta, AMJ, as his ... ers today call him, was also often talked of as ... Merchant Prince of Kenya''.

... an who rose from poverty in Karachi, where ... born in 1856, AMJ had a rare combination ... acious ambition which, coupled with an in... le entrepreneurial spirit, made him a man of ... wealth only years after his arrival in East ... . The energy he spared after long hours of ... ess activity was routinely expended in entero... g as well as in political and religious activism ... ade the pioneer economic giant also an icon ... colonial organisation.

... political standing of the man certainly ... endear him to the representatives of En-... 's Royal Court, nor did the cynicism with ... he garnished his rhetoric when criticising ... es he found unacceptable. The servants of his ... y could, however, simply not afford to ig-... MJ, and it is telling that for many years after ... ath, streets that had been named after him in ... asa and Nairobi kept AMJ's memory alive. ... ically, the streets — today Mwagozo in ... asa and Mfangano in Nairobi — were ... anised'' after independence.

... -humous honours aside, colonial figures ... ly showed more respect for AMJ in life than ... th, and their wariness of the man was certain-... y because of the awe in which they held him, ... because of his business acumen, subse-... economic clout and a penchant for lavish ... ing that saw many among the high and ... y in colonial circles dining at his expense.

I those invited to AMJ's receptions, dinners ... ties could expect gourmet fare, with all stops ... as far as expenses were concerned. At a par-... gave in May 1901 at the Grand Hotel in ... asa, the 50 guests savoured victuals that in-... caviar canapes and olives, pate de foie ... roasts and choice cheeses. The multi-... menu so impressed a journalist covering the ... on that his newspaper reported it alongside ... be's brow-raising report.

... most pleasant gathering was brought to a ... se in the small hours of the morning.... The ... le decorations were such as one would only ... ect at a first class Parisian Hotel, and aston-... ed every body (sic) that such perfection ... y place as British East Africa.

... very long after that reception, many admir-... re just as astonished as they watched their ... lowly slide towards bankruptcy, having lost ... wealth in deals that went awry either as a re-... sheer bad luck or suspected sabotage by ... titors too green-eyed to allow AMJ to soar ... higher in the commercial world.

... legendary entrepreneur had never been ... of envious watchers keen to clip his wings, ... nong them were even close members of his ... amily who took internecine feuds to rather

Alibhai Mulla Jeevanjee: "Probably had the single greatest impact on Kenya's social, political and economic history during the nearly five decades that he spent in the country."

astonishing extremes. But even more dangerous for the indefatigable investor were individuals or groups sworn to break his wings, so that they did not merely check his ascent, but also ensured his rapid economic descent.

This descent saw AMJ's lifestyle and that of his family plummet pathetically as old age caught up with him. From living in a regal two-storeyed villa surrounded by orchards and even having a cinema hall, the former mogul was to find himself living in very modest, almost pathetic, quarters on Park-lands' Second Avenue.

'The political standing of the man, certainly didn't endear him to the representatives of His Majesty's government, nor did his rhetoric when criticising their policies. They, however, could not afford to ignore him'

But people gathered at the National Museum last Friday for the launch of *Challenge to Colonialism: The Struggle of Alibhai Mulla Jeevanjee for Equal Rights in Kenya* were not wiping away tears, recalling the low tides in the pioneer's life; rather, they were celebrating the life of a man whose phenomenal rise to the apex of society became the stuff of legends.

The book, written by Jeevanjee's grand-daughter, Zarina Patel, is as unforgettable as the tumultuous times in which its subject lived. Its strength is its honesty and objectivity, both rare in biographies written by relatives. It captures the fury and

the sense of humour that AMJ alternated between, and captures the bravery of the man when his heels were dug in and his cudgels out in the anti-colonial war, as well as his remarkable stoicism when he was down and out economically.

Apart from the portrait of the man as a magnate who won all and lost all, there is the picture of the tireless crusader against injustice, a portly figure of deceptive humility who could cross swords with those in the top echelons of the colonial machine. Among them were Prime Ministers Lloyd George and Winston Churchill, whose power and

political stature did not deter AMJ from standing up to them and articulating his people's woes while also insisting that wrongs had to be righted.

Colonial governors in Kenya, opposed as they generally were to the excesses of settlers usually befuddled by arrogance and bigotry, did not find it easy to ignore AMJ's place in the country's political equation. Suffice it to say that they did not find it easy to ignore his social status either, and were often his satisfied guests.

But AMJ was not simply a buccaneer given to hedonistic living and political tantrums, and the biography brings out the pain he felt, for instance,

when he lost family members, or the joy he had as he, for instance, gave off a daughter in marriage.

As for his political vision, it certainly was not limited to agitation for Asian rights, and in many ways he was responsible, together with the late Isher Das, for cementing the ties between African nationalists and their Asian counterparts through close consultations with pioneer African political figures like Jesse Kariuki and Harry Thuku.

Although when he entered the Legislative Council it was principally to represent Asian interests and fight both racial and economic discrimination against Asians in the colony, AMJ had comrades across the colour line, and he constantly rubbed shoulders with all those who stood for justice and dignity.

In travels across four continents, AMJ had overcome the limitations brought about by his semi-illiteracy to become world-wise and it was not lost to him that the ideals for which the First World War had been fought had been lost sight of by the colonial powers. In a speech in Mombasa in December 1920, he noted that at the close of the war, many colonised people thought they had fought '' to establish for all time the freedom of all people to enjoy equal liberty and to determine their own destiny''.

These ideals had, however, been trampled underfoot by the colonial powers, who displayed such obvious double standards that AMJ was able to say, in reaction to the attitude of Lord Milner, the Secretary of State for the Colonies, that European settlers had to occupy prime land in Kenya's ''White Highlands'' not only from the sanitary point of view but as a matter of social convenience.

''Of course there is no discrimination in favour of the European,'' he hissed sarcastically. ''But I think we are entitled to say that when people come to settle in a land, they should study the convenience before they come and if there is anything that is not convenient to them they should stay away.''

It was not lost to him that the British colonialists viewed things through a different prism, and were prepared to stick to a policy of subjugating their subjects in the colonies to make life as comfortable as possible for their kith and kin.

''We know that is the position taken by the white communities of some of the self-governing colonies, people who are mighty particular about their rights when anybody comes into their country, whether by invitation or not, but thinking themselves free to invade other countries and enjoy therein superior rights to those of the inhabitants,'' he said.

The reactions of AMJ to such blatant abuses of power by the colonial authorities are core to the political message summarised in *Challenge to Colonialism*, which was described by Mr Pheroze Nowrojee, the guest of honour at the launch, as recording the man's social, economic and political achievements.

''But throughout it records the challenge to an unjust authority,'' said Mr Nowrojee. ''An authority that ruled without the consent of those it governed.''

Reading through the book, one gets the impression that anybody who attempted to humiliate Alibhai Mulla Jeevanjee came across those whose interests he was perpetually striving to articulate was in for a long-drawn and ferocious fight in which let-up would only be there if justice was done for all.

Portrait of Alibhai Mullah Jeevanjee in The Sunday Nation, *a Kenyan English-language newspaper, 14 December 1997. He wears a robe given to him by the Aga Khan.*

The Russian coachman

In 1826 the 6th Duke of Devonshire was sent on a special mission to Russia for the coronation of Tsar Nicholas. A coachman joined his staff while he was in residence in St Petersburg and returned to England with him. That Russian coachman, Peter Wisternoff, is our ancestor.

During his years at Chatsworth, in Derbyshire, Peter was paid £40 a year. He married a local girl, Sarah Newton, and they and their eight children lived in the ornate stables at Chatsworth, now a restaurant.

Peter was obviously a curiosity in the district. Georgiana Sitwell wrote:

'Another year we were taken to a concert at Chesterfield patronized by the Duke of Devonshire, who had just returned from his embassy to Russia ... and the Duke's coachman, with a very long beard (an

Cover of the 6th Duke's diary, showing Peter Wisternoff as coachman

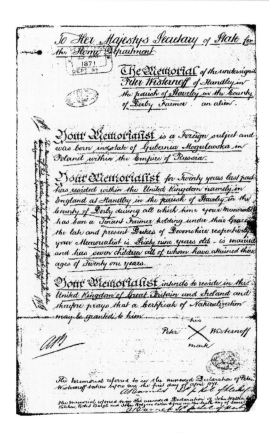

Peter Wisternoff's naturalisation application

appendage quite unknown in the England of those days), and in his native dress, sat in a prominent place and caused a great sensation.'

Princess Victoria recorded in her diary:

'Sat. Oct.20th 1832 – From there we went to the stables where we saw some pretty ponies and a Russian coachman in his full dress.'

After leaving Chatsworth in 1843 he lived near Chesterfield on the Duke's property until his death in 1878. He is buried with his wife at Spinkhill.

Today his descendants can be found in England, Wales, Canada, USA and New Zealand and are proud of their Russian ancestor.

Linda Perkins

A woman preacher

Jennie Buchan, my great-grandmother, was born in 1865 to a long line of Scottish crofters in Banffshire. She was one of seven in a close-knit Presbyterian family.

Jennie often told the story of when she was 19 and she and a friend walked 12 miles to a Sunday meeting in the town of Banff. They had heard about a strange religious movement that preached in military uniform. Jennie was shocked when she found them preaching in the street, but it was when she watched a young woman in a Salvation Army uniform actually praying in public that she began her transformation.

Jennie Buchan at the age of 30, and later in life in her coal-scuttle bonnet and with her family

Jennie made up her mind then to become a woman preacher – unheard of in northern Scotland. She tearfully left her disapproving family and all that was dear to her to give herself over to this evangelical movement.

While still in her early twenties Jennie was appointed personally by General William Booth to the 'mission field' in America. She left from Liverpool in 1891 with no luggage and landed in Cambridge, Massachusetts. Her preaching ability and Scottish brogue became legendary from Boston to Chicago, sometimes attracting thousands of listeners. Even well into her seventies she was being featured on the radio during Second World War broadcasts.

Her influence brought many people to follow in her footsteps, playing an important role in building the American Salvation Army as we know it today. To me, she was my great-grandmother. A special hero in a black, coal-scuttle bonnet.

Brad Hepburn

My brave aunt

This is the story of my aunt, Edith Nettleton, who went to China as a missionary and was murdered there by bandits.

Edith was born in Halifax in 1880, the second daughter in a working-class family of ten – seven girls and three boys. (My father, Edgar, was the youngest.) In 1890 she went to work in a local mill. She was a bright vivacious girl with a good sense of humour, always helping her mother and looking after the younger children. This training helped her in later life. She attended her local church and in September 1905 was accepted by the Church Missionary Society to train for work abroad.

Edith Nettleton. Her glasses provided a vital clue to the identity of her remains, which were found buried in the hillside in 1937 – the glasses case gave the name of her Halifax optician.

The Nettleton family in c. 1907, before Edith (right) went to China. Edgar, my father, is the small boy at the front.

On 3 November 1908, she arrived in Kien Yang, in Fukien Province, South China. She found she had an aptitude for languages and was soon fluent in both Mandarin and the local dialect. In 1910 she and Eleanor Harrison were posted to Chungan city, where Eleanor organised medical and educational work and Edith did social work.

From 1919–23 she was ill in England. On her return to China, things were very different – the Bolsheviks had been spreading anti-Christian propaganda. In January 1927 Edith and Eleanor were recalled to Kien Yang for safety, returning to Chungan in 1928. In 1930, they were again recalled because of fighting. While travelling down river, the ladies were captured by bandits and held hostage in a mountain shack. Ransom letters were sent, with Edith's little finger enclosed in one. The money was en route when they were beheaded and buried in the forest.

Joan Beaumont

The place for a village

This story concerns the founding of one of Australia's greatest cities.

William Batman was a Yorkshireman living in London who worked as a cutler and grinder. In 1796 he was found guilty at the Old Bailey of storing saltpetre stolen from the Crown; he was transported to Australia.

As William was considered to be of previously good character, his wife was allowed to accompany him at her own expense on a ship called *Ganges*.

They settled in Australia – in Parramatta near Sydney – and had several children, including one called John. Contemporary accounts suggest John was a good-looking man, adventurous and fond of women and alcohol.

John Batman

The record of William Batman's baptism on 9 April 1765, from the register at Hook Chapel

On 8 June 1835, John wrote in his journal: 'The boat went up the large river I have spoken of, which comes from the east, and I am glad to state, about six miles up found the river all good water and very deep. This will be the place for a village.'

And so the city of Melbourne was born.

John died of syphilis aged 39. The lives of William, my three-times-great-uncle, and his son John are well documented in Australian libraries. Today there is a statue of John in the centre of Melbourne and a separate monument that reads:

John Batman
Born at Parramatta N.S.W. 1800
Died at Melbourne 9 May 1839
He entered Port Phillips Heads 29 May 1835 as a leader of an expedition which he organized in Launceston V.D.L. to form a settlement and founded one on the site of Melbourne then unoccupied

This monument was erected by public subscription in Victoria.

Pat Cook

Kidnapped!

Great-uncle William John Charles Moens proposed to his wife on Hordle Cliffs, but, when she saw he had the ring ready in his pocket, she threw it into the sea and refused him for his presumption. She eventually agreed to marry in 1863. They undertook a Grand Tour for their honeymoon, but outside Paestum in Italy they were kidnapped by bandits.

William John Charles Moens

Aunt Annie was released, but he was held for two arduous months and forced to walk the mountains above Salerno. Uncle William attempted to escape but was always caught. He kept a Letts pocket diary secreted in the lining of his waistcoat in which he recorded everything. *The Times* of London reported it all, suggesting it was his own fault!

Poor Aunt Annie stayed in Naples, where she almost went mad with exasperation at the authorities. The bandits threatened to send her his ears in a box, if she did not secure the ransom. A relation from England eventually raised the money and travelled out to her. Half-starved, Uncle William was released. He wrote the story, combining his and his wife's diaries, and it was published in 1866. The proceeds from the book paid for the building of a school in Boldre, Hampshire.

David Manners

The Sea

The popular song exhorts Britannia to 'rule the waves'. Certainly, as befits an island nation, large numbers of our ancestors forged their livelihood from the sea. They fought to protect our shores as sailors with the Royal Navy, carried cargoes of exotic goods around the world as members of the merchant navy, or worked in support industries on shore, perhaps in dockyards or as part of a fishing community. Before the prevalence of commercial flight, the only way for our ancestors to travel around the British Empire was by ship.

One of the most famous passenger liners the world has seen was the ill-fated *Titanic*, and we have a tale from the descendant of a survivor that would not have been out of place in the film! Other stories in this section reflect a wide range of experiences of maritime life, including two accounts of the sinking of the *Lusitania* with different outcomes, and a display of heroism from a British sailor, who rescued a drowning enemy sailor during the Second World War. You can also find out how a bale of straw saved a man's life; the origins of the Birkenhead drill to evacuate women and children first from a sinking ship; and the amazing story of Toshie, the whaler.

Research Tips

Many of the stories featured in this section were drawn from family anecdotes passed down from generation to generation. However, if you suspect that you have ancestors who worked in a maritime industry, served with the Royal or merchant navy, or were involved in an incident on the high seas, you can conduct some research of your own. Service in the Royal Navy, as either an officer or rating, can be tracked via records at the National Archives, where you will also find historic material on the development of the Admiralty, ships logs and pay books, captains' letters, operational records from both world wars, and information on losses at sea. For civilian records there are ships' passenger lists from the late nineteenth century, plus material for the merchant navy that allows you to track basic career details.

The National Maritime Museum is another important resource, particularly if you want to investigate the wider context of Britain's role in the maritime community through the ages. Their research library contains original manuscripts that cover all aspects of commercial ships and shipping, plus a wealth of secondary source material. It is also important to explore resources at a local level.

Many crew lists and agreements have been deposited in local archives (with further material at the National Archives), and many maritime communities have well-stocked local study centres and museums that reflect life and times living with the sea through the ages. For additional reference, it might be worth consulting a journal called *Mariner's Mirror*, which contains numerous articles relating to Britain and the sea.

Escape from the Titanic

As a child I used to be taken to tea with my paternal grandparents, where boring family stories were related. However, there was one story that captured my imagination.

Jane Adelaide, sister of my grandfather, Robert Rowland, married an Italian, Louis Maioni. Their daughter, Roberta, was known as Cissy. At 18 Cissy began work as a lady's maid to the Countess of Rothes and escorted the Countess on the *Titanic*.

Simultaneously, my grandfather decided to take his only daughter, my aunt Ethel, to try his luck in Canada. Hearing about the *Titanic* crossing from Cissy, he tried unsuccessfully to book places in steerage. Instead they booked on the *Carpathia*.

Cissy Maioni (second from right), wearing the White Star badge

Telegram informing the family of Cissy's safety

Cissy and the Countess travelled first class. Cissy became friendly with a purser who gave her his White Star Line badge, which she wore on a chain round her neck. On that ill-fated night, Cissy and the Countess managed to get into one of the lifeboats. My grandfather told me that as Cissy rowed her long hair became entangled in the rowlocks. (Recently I communicated with the present Earl of Rothes, who has published a booklet in which he states his grandmother, the 'Plucky Countess', rowed the boat!)

Cissy was initially mistakenly reported as lost under the name of O'Mahoney. She and the Countess were picked up by the *Carpathia*, on which her uncle and cousin were travelling! Cissy wore the White Star badge constantly and was photographed wearing it at her brother's wedding.

My cousin, Alec Rowland, inherited the star from his mother, Jane Adelaide's sister, and in 1998 I saw it myself.

Beryl Roberts

£5 to buy some legs

In February 1884 the whaler, *Chieftain*, 150 tons register, set sail from Dundee for the Arctic. One of the men aboard was my great-grandfather, James McIntosh, known to his friends as 'Toshie'.

On 26 May, when a whale was sighted, four small boats were sent out after it. The whale was harpooned and took the boats a long way from the *Chieftain*. A fog came down and they were forced to cut the whale free. Now lost from the *Chieftain*, Toshie and the crew spent 17 days in an open boat in the North Sea. By the time they were picked up by a Danish shark fisher, Toshie was the only one alive.

James McIntosh,
1857–1919

Dundee Courier *report of*
James McIntosh's death

In the hospital at Aquereray a doctor stuck a long steel dagger into his foot, but Toshie felt no pain. During the amputation of both legs he remained conscious and saw his legs carried away. On his return to Dundee, Lord Derby sent him £5 to buy wooden legs. Toshie cycled to collect them from London on a tricycle especially adapted to be 'pedalled' with his hands; it took 20 days.

Many famous sea captains came to visit Toshie to hear his story, including Gellatly, Adams and of course, Scott, who was soon to die in his attempt to be the first to reach the South Pole.

Toshie went on to father ten children at his home at Broughty Ferry where he was employed as the railway-crossing keeper.

William McIntosh

Doubtful inheritance

When I was a young man I found some papers at home which intrigued me. It seemed that my uncle had discovered that the brother of his great-great-grandfather had left £1.5 million after his death at sea in about 1841. This money had been deposited in a bank in New Orleans.

After some initial enquiries he was told he would have to prove that he was, in fact, a direct descendant of this man before he could even try to claim his inheritance. This proved to be a daunting task! Some of the records were very difficult to find and he advertised in local papers for help in tracing members of the family who might have been able to help. Eventually it transpired that in order to get nearer to the source of the 'inheritance' he would have to go in person to the USA and continue his search there. He found out that this would be costly, and at the end of the day futile. At that point, he gave up the search.

However, as research had been started into our family history, one of my cousins has now traced the family back to 1564.

Finally, you may ask, how was this vast fortune amassed? I'm afraid I discovered that my ancestor had three ships and that he plied his trade in human cargo from Africa to America. He was a slave trader.

William Lamb

A Normandy landing

In January 1702 John Sandys, with seven other men and women, set off by open boat from Falmouth harbour intending to return home to St Keverne, a village on the Lizard, Cornwall, a journey of about three leagues. A storm blew up and they were blown before the wind for four days and nights, eventually landing on the coast of Normandy, 100 leagues from Falmouth.

We were at war with France, and on stepping ashore they were met by a group of armed Frenchmen. However, one of the Frenchmen had been shipwrecked at St Keverne; he remembered John Sandys and being treated well by him. Their arms and money were taken from them, including the 40 guineas John Sandys had been paid for pilchards at Falmouth. They were taken into custody as prisoners-of-war, and brought before a magistrate to be examined. He ordered them released and 'to beg the alms of the people'. John Sandys was taken in by the Frenchman who had been shipwrecked at St Keverne. They were all treated well.

News of their misadventure reached the ears of King Louis XIV, who ordered that they be put aboard the first transport ship of prisoners-of-war bound for England. On bidding farewell to his friend, John Sandys had his 40 guineas returned to him. They reached St Keverne about eight weeks after their departure from Falmouth, to the joy and astonishment of their friends and family who believed them drowned.

Helen Garrett

A life of service

Born in 1881, my grandfather, Harry James Usher, trained as a
shipwright at the Royal Navy Dockyard, Sheerness, in 1896; he joined
the Royal Navy in 1902.

Despite incurring 42 days' hard labour for jumping ship in Australia
in 1905, he went on to become a very disciplined and responsible
Warrant Officer.

Harry James Usher in 1918

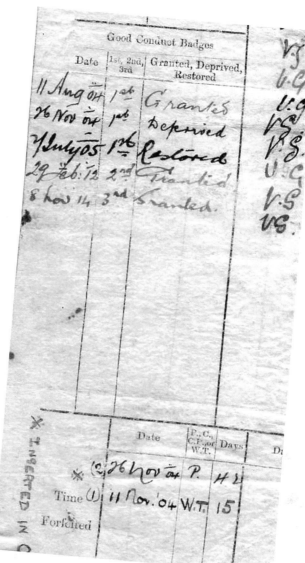

Extract from Harry's Royal Navy service record, showing the deprivation of his 1st Good Conduct Badge as a result of his dissertion and its subsequent restoration. The punishment for the offence, 42 days hard labour and the loss of 15 days' wages, appears at the foot.

With the advent of military aviation, he transferred to the Royal Flying Corps (Naval Wing), later to become the Royal Naval Air Service in 1914. This marked the beginning of a lifetime career in waterborne aviation.

Harry and his wife and daughter near Salonika in Greece in 1930. Moored in the background is the Imperial Airways Short Calcutta flying boat, 'City of Athens'.

In 1918 the RNAS became the RAF, and he found himself wearing RAF blue and far removed from the service he had originally joined. Although unhappy with this, he became a Flying Officer in the embryonic RAF where, with his experience of marine aircraft, he was posted to the Marine Aircraft Experimental Establishment at RAF Felixstowe in 1924.

He was twice seconded to the High Speed Flight which, with Gloster III and Gloster IV racing seaplanes, contested the 1925 and 1927 Schneider Trophy races.

In 1929 he left the RAF and joined Imperial Airways, the forerunner of today's British Airways, operating flying boat passenger services out of Salonika in Greece and Alexandria in Egypt, where he and my grandmother lived until his sudden death in 1932.

As a member of the RAF myself, I'm sad that I never had the privilege of meeting him, but in 1982, with the assistance of diplomatic records, I located his grave at Camp Caesar in Alexandria.

Stuart Usher

Women and children first

My great-grandfather, James Boyden, was born in Ireland in 1830 and emigrated to America with his parents and family. In 1850 he returned and joined the British Army. After five months' service in the 2nd Foot Regiment, James sailed from Ireland in 1852 on board the *Birkenhead* en route to the Kaffir Wars in South Africa. The ship was an iron paddle steamer of 1,400 tons carrying reinforcements for the regiments involved in the Kaffir Wars.

Suddenly, in the early hours of 26 February 1852, there was a grinding crash. The ship had struck a submerged rock near Dangerpoint, 50 miles from Simonstown, South Africa, and ripped a hole beneath her waterline. Many soldiers drowned in their bunks – the rest stood firm as the women and children were placed into the only lifeboats that could be launched. Thus began the tradition of 'women and children first' – otherwise known as the 'Birkenhead Drill'. The ship finally sank and the men were left to save themselves. Nearly 450 soldiers and seamen died but, thanks to their steadfastness, not one woman or child was lost.

James survived by getting hold of a truss of hay that was floating in the water: he was carried into the shore by the current. Another survivor passing by shouted 'come on Jack Straw', and that nickname stuck with James throughout his regimental career. Many years have passed since this event but family historians like myself have reason to be proud of their kin who took part in this great and moving tragedy.

Eileen Combellack

Lost on the Lusitania

'Old Head of Kinsale, May 7, 2.45 p.m. Steamer Lusitania – sunk by submarine 2.33 p.m. eight miles south by west. Calm.' *Lloyds List.*

My mother's cousin Ida Exley was the daughter of Joseph, a wool sorter. His wife Annie, Ida and her two brothers lived comfortably in the Yorkshire village of Saltaire and Joseph deliberated for many years before deciding to join his brother in Massachusetts. The two families settled in neighbouring farms at Barre.

The Exley family – Ida is the child at the front of the photograph

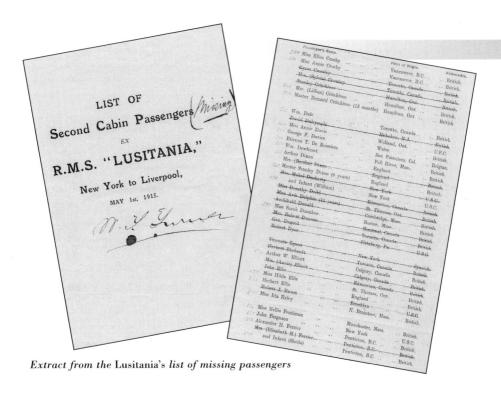

Extract from the Lusitania's *list of missing passengers*

Ida was a lively teenager. She became infatuated with Harry Taylor, who returned to Yorkshire to set up a decorator's business. In spite of the war in Europe, Ida determined to follow him.

Against all the pleas of her family, she booked a passage on the *Lusitania*. The German Embassy in Washington had issued a warning that the ship, said to be carrying ammunition, was a likely target for U-Boat torpedoes. Ida is said to have laughed, 'If one end of the ship sinks, I'll run up the other end'.

No trace of her, or the trousseau she had packed with such excitement, was ever recovered. Apparently her second-class berth was in direct line with the torpedo. Ida was just 18 years of age.

When the news reached Barre, seven of Ida's friends (members of the cricket team) downed tools and sailed for England, intent on taking the King's shilling to avenge the untimely death of Ida Exley.

Sylvia Brooks

Rescued from the Lusitania

Rose Howley went to New York to visit her niece. On 1 May 1915 she boarded the *Lusitania* to return to England. On Friday, 7 May, the ship was making its way towards Ireland and at about 2 p.m. Rose was walking on deck with a friend when suddenly there was an almighty explosion. A German U-Boat had torpedoed the *Lusitania*.

The two ladies managed to get to where the lifeboats were being launched. People were panicking and screaming. Rose spotted a rope and slid down it into the sea. She had lost her friend by this time. The ship was sinking rapidly and twice she was drawn under by the suction. When she came up she felt a hard surface: it was an overturned lifeboat, to which three men were already clinging.

Rose Howley, 1866–1945

CHILD CLINGING TO HER DRESS

While she had been endeavouring to get a firm hold of the boat Mrs. Howley had felt something tugging at her dress, and looking round she noticed a little girl. She exclaimed: "Oh! its a child" and with the assistance of the men the girl was pulled up as well. Mrs. Howley then recognised her as Edith Williams, one of a family with whom she had become acqainted on the ship. There were the mother, five girls, and a boy, and only the boy and Edith were saved. The group clung to the boat for four hours before assistance reached them. Two other of the ship's boats came near and linked themselves with the upturned boat. They did what was possible to rescue those straggling around, and two women were taken up in a very exhausted condition. At length a steamer was seen approaching, and a man in one of the boats hoisted a portion of his clothing on the end of an oar and signalled for help, while the people in the boats shouted as hard as possible.

An extract from Keighley News, *15 May 1915*

They managed to pull her partly into the boat and while she was trying to get a hold she felt something tugging on her skirt. It was a little girl, Edith Williams. She was also pulled onto the boat and Rose looked after her. After some time they were finally rescued and taken to Queenstown.

Edith's family tried to get in touch with Rose to thank her for saving Edith's life, but Rose was a private person and did not respond. She felt she didn't need thanking.

I have recently been in touch with Edith's son, who passed on thanks after 88 years! Rose Howley was my great-great-aunt on my father's side of the family.

Catherine Higgs

Trapped in the ice

My great-grandfather, Joseph Bayley, was the youngest of six children. Like his older brothers and father, he was a seafarer, and like them he rose to become a captain.

In 1894 he joined the *Windward* as first mate. *Windward* was the supply ship for the Jackson-Harmsworth expedition which aimed to explore and map Franz Josef Land. Leaving London in July 1894, the plan was to transport Jackson's team and equipment, and return to England before winter. After some setbacks, they only reached Franz

Officers of the Windward, *with Joseph Bayley in the middle of the front row*

Josef Land by September; within days the weather changed and winter set in. The *Windward* was trapped in ice, and Jackson's party of seven unexpectedly escalated to 40, forced to spend the winter at the small Arctic campsite.

These cold dark days of winter are recorded in both Joseph Bayley's diary and Jackson's book, *1000 Days in the Arctic*. At great risk, they shot polar bears, seals and birds for food. The families at home probably feared the worst when the *Windward* failed to return.

Only in July 1895 did the ice break up sufficiently to start the return journey. This was also eventful and dangerous: the crew encountered thick ice, suffered an outbreak of scurvy and ran out of coal, which meant burning some wooden parts of the ship as fuel.

The *Windward* eventually arrived off Norway in the middle of September. When she reached London she had to be rebuilt before returning to Franz Josef Land in both 1896, taking part in the famous rescue of Nansen, and 1897, setting a new record in Arctic voyages.

Angela Beale

A telegram from Churchill

My uncle was Lieutenant E. Burkitt, known as Peter, a secretary to Captain Vian in the Royal Navy. He was on board HMS *Cossack* in 1940 when 300 British prisoners were rescued from the *Altmark*, a German merchant ship.

It was the last time men from a British ship ever boarded another ship. This is well documented as the 'Altmark incident'.

My uncle did something that day which is not as well documented but was incredibly brave. He dived into the water to save a German sailor who had fallen in. Churchill laughed uproariously when he heard about the rescue and sent a telegram congratulating the ship's crew on having saved 300 British prisoners and a German from drowning on the same day.

The Altmark's *mouthpiece from the bridge of the ship, which Peter Burkitt took as a souvenir.*

FROM.   CAPTAIN(D).IV.

TO.   ARETHUSA, COSSACK, IVANHOE, INTREPID,
           SIKH, NUBIAN.

Following from First Lord, begins -

"The Force under your orders is to be
congratulated on having in a single day achieved
the double rescue of Britons from captivity and
Germans from drowning."

(T.O.O.2149/17/2.)

Ends.

This message refers to the rescue of the crew
after scuttling of the German Tanker BALDUR, by H.M. Ships
IVANHOE and INTREPID, and to the rescue of a German
sailor at great risk to themselves by two officers of
H.M.S.COSSACK.

1023/18/2/39.

Auth.

The original telegram received from Churchill, congratulating the Cossack *crew*

We have the soldier's identity bracelet, a piece of the *Altmark* ship and Churchill's telegram. I have also written up the whole story. My uncle never got a medal because there are no medals given in war for saving one of the enemy!

Richard Burkitt

One of those twists of fate

It never ceases to amaze me how those little twists of fate can have such a dramatic effect on a family's history.

My grandfather, Albert Matthews, was handed over to relatives in 1897 when he was just four years old. Almost an orphan, he joined the Navy when he was a boy and reached the rank of Stoker Petty Officer on HMS *Valerian* when he was 33.

On the fateful day, 22 October 1926, the *Valerian* was sunk in a hurricane off Bermuda. Out of the entire crew only Albert and 11 other men survived. They made a raft from pieces of the ship and spent 22 hours in the water before, exhausted, they were picked up by the *Cape Town*.

All 12 survivors from the Valerian. My grandfather, Albert Matthews, is standing at the centre

Considering Albert's job was in the boiler room it was a sheer miracle he survived. If he had not, my dad – born more than two years later – would never have existed and nor, therefore, would I.

Albert retired from the Navy in the mid 1930s, but on the outbreak of the Second World War he joined the merchant navy and served on the Atlantic convoys. He died in 1969 when I was just three so I barely remember him. All I have are his medals, naval record and a piece of a Carley Float – a sort of life raft – that he and the rest of the survivors divided between them, so that they would remember the *Valerian* and all their mates who didn't make it.

Ross Matthews

The family bible

As a police officer I have often sworn on the bible, but you might have forgiven me when I saw this one. Its contents could have saved me years researching my Cornish roots!

On New Year's Eve 1821, John Spear Trescowthick, 28 years, drowned near Bedruthen Steps. A huge wave swept him off a rock near a shipwreck. John's family, including his daughter, Maria, moved to Crugmeer, next door to his brother Philip, a stonemason and well-known local character. He carved John's headstone, which is in Padstow churchyard.

Samuel Alford

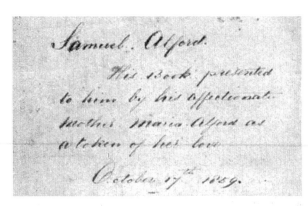

Through the present owners of Philip's cottage, I now have photos of Philip and family and copies of family letters he wrote to New Zealand, kept by a descendant there. Fragments of a newspaper dated 1863 were found in a fireplace at the cottage.

John's daughter, Maria, married William Alford, a Padstow shipwright whose ancestors were fishermen, seaman, farm labourers and smugglers from Port Isaac. His great-great-grandfather was killed in a famous sea battle in 1758 on HMS *Monmouth* when it took a French ship, *Foudroyant*.

Padstow dockyard declined and William and Maria moved to Woolwich dockyard, Kent. Samuel Alford was their son. I descend from his second wife, Katherine Bachelor. Unbeknown to me until recently, Samuel later married Katherine's sister Sarah and had more children. One descendant gave me photos of Maria and Samuel – and she also has Maria's family bible, given to Samuel in 1859. Maria and Samuel wrote family events in it in great detail. Shame I hadn't seen it earlier!

John Alford

Enterprise and Discovery

In this selection, we commemorate the unsung men and women whose contributions, ideas and inventions over the centuries have not captured the headlines. A perfect example is the story of the clerk working for Bass, who queued all night outside the patent office to ensure the famous 'Red Triangle' became the trademark for the brewery. There are astonishing stories of exploration, where our ancestors fearlessly ventured into the unknown in a quest for knowledge and understanding. Others had minor roles in momentous historical events, such as the doctor who accompanied the reporter Stanley on his quest to find the missionary Livingstone in Africa.

There are inspirational tales of perseverance, such as that of William Bray. His designs for a traction engine were rejected in Britain, largely due to the prominence of the railways. In order to follow his dream he relocated his family to St Petersburg and assisted with the modernisation of Russia but the 1917 revolution forced his descendants to return to Britain.

Perhaps the most remarkable story is that of William Paterson, whose work with the humble potato during the time of the famine preserved the species from possible extinction and thereby saved countless lives. On a more bizarre level, you can read about the man who – literally – shook hands with his four-times-great-grandfather who had been dead for one-and-a-half centuries.

Research Tips

The diverse world of enterprise and invention will lead the researcher to rather more specialised archives. Many of the stories featured here were researched using the archives of organisations such as the Royal Geographical Society. You may also find deposited papers, manuscripts and contemporary accounts of inventors and their inventions in places such as the Institute of Civil Engineers. Many designs and representations were initially filed with the Board of Trade, and you can see specifications, samples, sketches and early patent applications at the National Archives. Later patents, plus trademark registrations, are with the British Library.

You should also see if any working papers of the companies and businesses where your ancestors worked survive in county archives or among separate business archives. It is also worth checking to see if any of the relevant societies and institutions publish their own journals, as you are likely to find information about the work of your relatives even if they did not find prominence in the wider world.

On a more general level it is still worth trawling through newspaper coverage of the day, either regional papers, where important contributions to the local economy are likely to be featured, or national titles where feats of exploration, bravery and scientific discovery may appear. Indeed you may be lucky enough to find an obituary notice recounting some of the deeds of your forebears.

Saviour of the potato

My great-great-grandfather, William Paterson, has had little recognition for his work to save the potato from extinction. Archibald Findlay, in a lecture in Glasgow in 1905, said: 'I did not have the good fortune to know William Paterson. But I will say this – his potato, the 'Victoria', was about the biggest gift ever bestowed on the human race.'

Born in Dundee in 1808, William Paterson had a flourishing market garden. From 1826 he noticed a weakening in the potato plant. This was the start of the famous blight which affected most parts of Great Britain and Ireland. He spent 40 years experimenting to produce a healthy plant, using samples from all over the world.

The Victoria potato was born using the seeds taken from the 'apple' formed after the potato flower has died. In his words, 'the benefit to society has been attained at very considerable pecuniary loss to myself' – a reported £7,000. Paterson's Victoria became universally famous and even Queen Victoria wrote personally to order seedlings for Windsor (we have an order in her handwriting).

William's work particularly benefited the Irish, whose diet depended on the potato. We don't think the projected Irish memorial materialised, but he received

William Paterson

One of the tributes received by William for his work with the potato – a solid silver epergne in the shape of a potato plant, awarded by the landowners of Forfarshire

many other awards, including the Erfurt Medal and Diploma of Honour as saviour of the potato in Europe in 1865. The most beautiful is a solid silver epergne in the shape of a potato plant, presented by landed proprietors, farmers and potato merchants of Forfarshire, which is still in the family.

He gave much of his life to save this valuable commodity but after he died in 1870 he sank into oblivion.

Heather Byrne

The traction engine

A traction engine that could haul loads over any surface was the dream of my great-great-grandfather William Bray. He was a marine engineer who transferred his expertise in paddle steamers to the land. His invention was a mechanism with adjustable teeth that gave the portion of the drive wheels in contact with the ground a good purchase, but slid back into the rim as the wheel turned.

The patent traction engine – William Bray is the figure in the top hat

In 1858 his traction engine was featured in the *Illustrated London News*. The photograph opposite shows him, the personification of the confident Victorian entrepreneur in a top hat, standing proudly on his traction engine with two of his sons. One Bray traction engine was the first motorized road vehicle in Australia, and another was the highlight of a touring American Circus. One machine, hauling a 22 ton load to Woolwich Dockyard, broke through the roadway and fell into the cellars below.

William Bray's engine was not a commercial success in England because of the spread of railways and better roads. However, the Russian authorities saw its usefulness, and in 1867 William moved his large family to St Petersburg. His brother and sons stayed in Russia, and eventually three generations of Brays lived and worked in St Petersburg, helping Russia modernize in the second half of the nineteenth century.

William's grandson, Walter (my grandfather), lived on Kristofskoye Island in the Lena River, and his first son was born there just weeks before the 1917 Revolution. In 1918, all the Brays fled the Bolsheviks and returned to England.

Adrian Bray

An intrepid explorer

My ancestor was a Swiss–German explorer, Jean Louis Burckhardt. He was born in Basle in 1784, the son of a wealthy merchant and patrician soldier. He was indefatigable but unassuming and utterly dedicated. Gifted in languages and music, he made himself into a liberal humanist. He loved the simplicity of the desert compared to towns. He was a great admirer of England and was a most notable traveller in the early days of African exploration.

Jean Louis Burckhardt by H. Salt in 1817, from the original published diaries, showing him in an Arab bernous

It was through Sir Joseph Banks he undertook to spend two-and-a-half years studying. He lived as an Arab in Aleppo and travelled into the desert between 1809 and 1817. The year of Bonaparte's retreat from Moscow saw the start of Louis's first long journey to Cairo, at great personal danger, through Syria and ultimately to Jordan where he discovered Petra. This was a mission on behalf of London's Africa Association, later to be incorporated in the Royal Geographical Society. Louis also travelled down the Nile and into unexplored territory: he found the Great Temple of Ramases II at Abu Sinbel which was buried in sand.

He was always in danger and often in great discomfort. He was very modest and most surprised at the praise he received, which may be why he is not better known today.

James Burckhardt

Exploration and espionage

My great-great-grandfather was Major Robert Gill, employed by the East India Company to record the fabulous cave temple paintings at Ajanta, north-west India. He also pioneered stereo photography of mid-nineteenth century India.

I am descended from his daughter via a mistress that he had while resident in India. Her half-brother (my great-great-uncle) was the explorer William Gill. He came into a fortune and, instead of spending it on wine, women and song, used it to finance expeditions of geographical exploration combined with undercover espionage for Queen and country. He was, in effect, Queen Victoria's answer to David Attenborough and James Bond rolled into one.

Hand-coloured photo on glass of Major Robert Gill, now owned by my mother and Gill's great-granddaughter, Winefride Hadland

THE LATE CAPTAIN W. GILL, R.E.

Robert Gill's logo, found on the back
of one of the many photographs he
took

Line drawing of Robert Gill's famous son,
the explorer and spy William Gill, which
appeared in the Brighton College magazine
in 1882

William Gill's journeys took him to Tibet, China, India, Burma, Persia, Turkey, North Africa, the Middle East and the Balkans. He helped settle a border dispute between Turkey and Russia. The Royal Geographical Society and its French equivalent both awarded him gold medals for his achievements.

When the nationalist revolt took place in Egypt, William Gill was sent there as an intelligence officer. He was sent to cut the telegraph lines between Constantinople and Alexandra to stop the rebels gaining information detrimental to the British. Although travelling in disguise as an Arab, he was betrayed and, with his colleagues, murdered in the Sinai Desert.

He is buried in St Paul's Cathedral, London, and commemorated in Rochester Cathedral, Kent.

Anthony Hadland

The stained-glass window

Intriguingly my late grandmother told me that there was a stained-glass window in a church in Nottingham dedicated to my three-times-great-grandfather, Thomas Whiteley (1790–1860). Unfortunately she never gave me the details of where the church was and after she died its whereabouts remained a mystery. All I knew was that Thomas Whiteley was a lace manufacturer.

Inspired by this competition I decided to find the whereabouts of this church. Through the internet I contacted the Local Studies Library in Nottingham which explained that Thomas Whiteley invented many improvements to lace machines in the nineteenth century. Next I

The stained-glass window at St Helen's church in Stapleford

The exterior of St Helen's

spoke to a lace historian who told me that Thomas Whiteley's factory used to be in a suburb of Nottingham called Stapleford. Now I was able, from my home in Glasgow, to trace the church on the web. The website of St Helen's church in Stapleford has this to say:

'Above the communion table is a beautiful East Window ... It bears the inscription "Dedicated to the memory of his father, Thomas Whiteley, who largely contributed to the development of the lace trade in this place, by John Whiteley and Mary Ann his wife. AD 1877".'

I was overjoyed! At last the mystery of the window's whereabouts was uncovered. Now I finally knew the exact details of the famous stained-glass window that Grandma had so often referred to. My next trip will be to St Helens at Stapleford to honour my locally famous ancestor!

Vicki Mckenna

Shaking hands with an ancestor

Jean Baptiste Benjamin Godin attended the French church, named 'La Patente', which occupied the house next door to his in Brown Lane, but he was buried in the crypt of nearby Christ Church, Spitalfields, London, on 29 September 1829. He lay in the darkness for about 155 years, undisturbed by events in the outside world. Then during an archaeological dig known as the Spitalfields Project his remains were excavated in 1984–5, and shortly thereafter stored for posterity.

Thus my ancestor now finds himself in a cardboard box in the Natural History Museum. In October 1998 I paid a visit to that revered establishment, and was fortunately permitted to look upon the last remains of my direct ancestor. The bones were dark with age and from long exposure to the dirt and filth in the burial chamber. Among the bones in the larger box there was a small plastic envelope in which I could see a number of very small bones.

On my asking about this small plastic container, I was told me that these were finger bones, which were kept separately because they were so small. I realized that in my hand I was holding the hand of Jean Baptiste. Not many people can say that they have held the hand of an ancestor from so many generations before their own. Then I waved the little bag back and forth a little, and that is how I shook the hand of my four-times-great-grandfather.

Chris Shelley

Great-great-uncle's medallion

A few years back, while working as an accountant at the Wellcome Foundation (now part of Glaxo Wellcome), my late wife Alice was looking through some family memorabilia. She pointed out that a silver medallion presented to my great-great-uncle, Thomas Parke, had the word 'Wellcome' in small letters engraved on the side.

Further rummaging through family documents identified from an old banquet menu that Henry S. Wellcome, the founder of Burroughs and Wellcome (to become the Wellcome Foundation) had designed the medal. At around the same time I heard an old recording on a wax cylinder from the BBC archives of H. M. Stanley, the explorer who

The medallion presented by the Americans in London society to all expedition members including Thomas Parke

rescued Livingstone, speaking at the Lord Mayor of London's dinner in his and the expedition's honour in 1891. 'Uncle Tom' – Thomas Parke – was the doctor on Stanley's expedition (the Emin Pasha Expedition).

Within a couple of months the connection was featured in the company magazine. The 'final clincher' came a few weeks later when a warehouseman in Dartford where I worked showed me a newspaper article, dated 1891, he had just found in the store describing the same dinner.

Thomas Parke

Stanley's watch, which in 1887 was given in pledge to the Manyuema chief for the services of guides to lead Stanley out of the Manyuema territory during the African expedition. The watch was redeemed in 1888 and given to Parke with the inscription: 'To surgeon T. H. Parke as a souvenir of Fort Bodo and Ipoto, 1887 and 1888, from his friend Henry M. Stanley'. Thomas described the date of the gift as 'one of the brightest hours of my life'.

This has inspired me to do a lot more research in the years since. I have discovered that not only was Stanley my grandfather's godfather, but the Irish Parke family still have a castle named after them, now in ruins. The coat of arms over the castle entrance shows that they originally came from Sutton Valence in Kent around 1600.

Chris Stoker

'I will hold my station to the last'

My great-grandfather, John Edward Todhunter, was a Deputy
Superintendent of Telegraphs in India, helping to install the first
telegraph system in the North Western Provinces in the Agra area,
when the Indian Mutiny started in 1857. Aged 29, he joined the
Voluntary Services, to assist in re-establishing the telegraph system
after rebel forces cut the wires to stop communication. This he
achieved with two other men, as detailed in a minute by the Governor

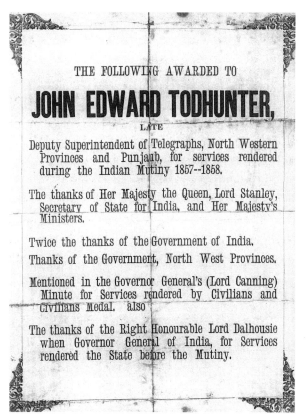

THE FOLLOWING AWARDED TO

JOHN EDWARD TODHUNTER,

LATE

Deputy Superintendent of Telegraphs, North Western
Provinces and Punjaub, for services rendered
during the Indian Mutiny 1857--1858.

The thanks of Her Majesty the Queen, Lord Stanley,
Secretary of State for India, and Her Majesty's
Ministers.

Twice the thanks of the Government of India.

Thanks of the Government, North West Provinces.

Mentioned in the Governor General's (Lord Canning)
Minute for Services rendered by Civilians and
Civilians Medal, also

The thanks of the Right Honourable Lord Dalhousie
when Governor General of India, for Services
rendered the State before the Mutiny.

The citation from Queen
Victoria

John Edward Todhunter

General, Lord Canning, which states that: 'restoration has been accomplished with extraordinary rapidity, using copper wire, odds and ends of wire from the roadside and bazaars, branches from trees and bamboos not more substantial than walking sticks. Mr Todhunter worked from Indore, opening offices at Beowra, Buzeud, Ragoohur and Goona – this while officially warned to quit the line by both Sir Robert Hamilton and myself – his answer was, "I am well mounted and well armed and I will hold my station to the last" ... He kept his word.'

An earlier report by his Superintendent states, 'He saved all his instruments and public property in his office at Agra but there and at Indore lost all the private property he possessed. He has been thanked by the Government and promoted in the department. He has since, through his indomitable courage and untiring exertions, reconstructed the Indore and Agra line [approx 375 miles] in the presence of rebel cavalry'.

John Edward Todhunter was awarded a civilian medal and citation giving him the thanks of Queen Victoria, her ministers and the government of India.

Tony Todhunter

Scottish pride

Most of my maternal ancestors were miners working in various parts of the Lothians. The earliest that we have traced is James Pride, born around 1678 and thirled (bound) to the Laird of Prestongrange. A cousin who lived in Wales discovered that the National Library of Scotland held a journal which recorded a few years in the 1740s of the work carried out in the Prestongrange mine and saltpans. As I live in Bo'ness, I went to have a look at this journal and found James and his sons mentioned quite frequently.

This was a wonderful find in itself, but just as I was about to hand the journal back I discovered a pocket in the back with some loose papers in it. One of the sheets provided the real find of the day! It was

The petition to the Laird of Prestongrange, with transcription (trustees of the National Library of Scotland)

a petition which had been drawn up for James, two of his sons (one of whom is my direct ancestor) and two other men. They begged the Laird of Prestongrange not to lend them to the Duke of Hamilton for his mine at Borrowstowness (the full name of the Bo'ness) as the men there had threatened them if they took the bread from their mouths.

Unfortunately I have no means of knowing whether or not this petition was successful. At the time it was drawn up James was about 70 so I really hope he was left to finish his years at peace in his own home.

Hetty Bennie

Unto ye Honourable ye Lord Grang at Prestongrange.
ye Petition of Robert Pryde, James Pryde his son, James Pryde, Robert Thomson and William Ines all Colzers [*Colliers*] belonging to his Lordship

Humbly Sheweth
That we all are your Lordships servants and is willing to serve your Lordship qn yt [*when that*] you have work for us But since yt [*that*] your Lordships work is not goeing at Prestongraing we at ye [*the*] tyme is at Pinky [?] under Mr Robertson and not far from your Lordship so yt qn yt [*so that while yet*] you are pleased to fit your work in Presongraing we are near to be gotten qn yt [*when that*] your Lordship pleases

And at ye tyme John Birel, Overseman to ye duke of Hameltown is hard upon us in stoping us of bread where we now are be [*by*] lifting us out of ys [*this*] work to place us in ye Lo [*Lord*] Dukes work at Bowersstness [*Borrowstounness*]

And now ye workmen yt is there sweres yt if yt we go to yt work yt they shall be our dead [*And now the workmen that is there swears that if that we go to that work that they shall be our dead*]

And now we humbly Prey yt [*that*] you out of your Clemcncy & goodness will keep us from goeing to yt [*that*] place where out life will be in so much danger; And we your Lordships humble petitioners shall ever pray

Robert Pried
mark of James Pryd
mark of James Pride
mark of Rott Thomson [*Robert Thomson*]
mark of William Ines

Back to the drawing board

As a young designer at the ceramic company, W. T. Copeland and Sons (Spode), my grandfather, Harold Holdway, was frustrated that after his art-school training he was not being given many chances to prove himself. In 1938, the firm's American agent came on his annual trip to select new designs. The designers were ordered to develop some of his suggestions; if their design was rejected they were reprimanded by the

The original Christmas Tree pattern sketch by Harold Holdway, © The Holdway Family

art director, but if the design proved pleasing, they were greeted with 'well, why in hell's name didn't you come up with that before?'

This time my grandfather was asked to design something for the Christmas market. He went back to his desk and drew a Christmas tree with presents hanging from the branches and showed it to the agent for approval. He approved but said there was something wrong: 'In the States, we put presents around the base of the tree, not on the branches'. As my grandfather's family were too poor to have a Christmas tree, he had not known what they were meant to look like!

So it was back to the drawing board. Samples were sent to America but that was nearly the end of the story. At the last minute the agent got cold feet, but his sales staff, who loved the design, persuaded him otherwise. The design became a great success, so much so that it has been in continuous production ever since, celebrating its 65th anniversary this year. Spode estimate the pattern is now in 10 million US homes.

Ruth Holdway

Britain's oldest trademark

Standing next to the champagne, two bottles of Bass Ale are prominent features in Edouard Manet's painting of *The Bar at the Folies-Bergeres*. By 1882, when the painting was first exhibited, the Bass Red Triangle was an easily recognised trademark, not only in this country but also in many other parts of the world. It had been used on labels for pale ale as early as 1855 and helped Bass to become one of the first companies to establish a brand image.

In order to give owners of trademarks legal protection against copying and forgery, the Trade Marks Registration Act was introduced in 1875. A member of the Bass staff spent an uncomfortable night on the steps of the Registrar's office in London to gain first entry when it opened for the first time on 1 January 1876. He was rewarded with the No. 1 registration for the Bass Red Triangle, which has become Britain's oldest registered trademark.

George Myott started work with the Bass Company in 1868 as a junior clerk. When he retired in 1914, he had risen through the ranks to become company secretary. As testimony to his esteem in Burton-on-Trent, where the company was based, his obituary was the lead article in the *Burton Daily Mail*.

George Myott was my great-grandfather and reputedly the member of the Bass staff who slept on the steps of the Registrar's office. Every time I drink a pint of Bass, I remember his role in securing the world-famous Red Triangle.

David Myott

A beer pump handle showing the Bass Red Triangle secured by George Myott in 1876. This famous trademark is now the property of the Belgian brewing company, Interbrew, and the Bass brewery is now owned by the American giant, Coors. What will be the fate of the Red Triangle?

The mad dog

Robert Holmes was a police officer and, like many others in the Force, had quite an adventurous life. One particular event has remained in family memory. While on duty, Robert encountered a boy being savaged by a dog. In the style of the age, Robert cut through the throng of by-standers and succeeded in saving the boy from further injury. However, Robert himself was bitten quite severely.

What adds interest to this 'dog bites man' story is that the dog was rabid, and at the time rabies was fatal. It transpired that the boy's family was not without financial means and that the Pasteur Institute in Paris was conducting research into this horrible disease. The injured boy's family learned of this research and paid for their son and his rescuer, my great-great-uncle, to be taken to Paris for the still experimental treatment – which proved successful. Robert became the 'first Brit' to be cured of rabies.

Robert was born in 1843 in Glentham, Lincolnshire, the son of George and Mary. He married Ann and they had two daughters and three sons. After retirement, Robert joined his brother, Adam, my great-grandfather, in Sheffield. Robert's children were Mary (b.1865), Elizabeth (b.1879), George (b.1865), Wilkinson (b.1868) and Robert (b.1868). Adam and his wife, Mary Surfleet, had four sons and four daughters.

Keith Lainton

Robert Holmes,
c. 1896

Hard Times

It can be easy to forget how hard life was for our ancestors. Better public sanitation, advances in medicine and a varied and bountiful diet have improved our standard of living beyond all recognition compared to conditions in the middle of the nineteenth century. Then cholera epidemics swept the land, unemployment often equalled starvation or life in the workhouse, and the potato famine crippled Ireland's economy.

The stories featured in this section emphasise the fact that, as genealogists, we are researching real people, whose lives were touched by tragedy on a daily basis. Included is a moving inscription in a family bible, letters written to a prisoner-of-war about the birth of a child whom he never saw, and a woman clawed to death by a bear that was being kept for baiting.

One impoverished family were packed off to Australia so that they were no longer a burden on their parish. A woman visited a chemist's store to buy medicine for her children, but picked up the wrong package – with disastrous results.

These are the forgotten stories, but one contributor was amazed to discover that the death of one of his relatives had been immortalised in verse and paint!

Research Tips

It is easy to overlook the 'cause of death' on an official certificate, especially if you are initially looking for genealogical information. However, as some of the stories show, the cause of death often gives you an important insight into the more unusual fates that befell our ancestors. Some of the terms used on the death certificate are clearly technical, and you need the help of a medical dictionary to decipher them, but if a more tragic or unusual cause of death was recorded, it is highly likely that an official coroner's inquest was held before the certificate could be issued. The best place to start looking for records of coroner's inquests is your county record office, but survival rates are not good. However, many unusual cases were also reported in the local newspapers, so once you have a firm date of death it should be easy to track down any reports that were published.

You can also use occupation data, obtained from certificates or census returns, to provide social and economic context to your relatives, and therefore begin to come to conclusions about whether they were living through hard times. Different occupations and regions have experienced varying levels of success and failure since the Industrial Revolution changed British society in the late eighteenth century. You might want to focus on the main employer in the region and see if there are any staff records, or perhaps consider whether the industry experienced a period of decline while your relatives were alive. If they were affected by unemployment or poverty, it might be worth examining poor relief records or even workhouse registers, which (if they survive) are likely to be deposited in the relevant county record office.

A Hando child

'Another pair of shoes for a Hando child.' This entry in the parish poor relief record was probably the last straw.

Generations of Handos struggled against rural poverty in Victorian Somerset. They drifted to nearby towns in search of work – Bridgwater, Taunton, Bristol and South Wales.

William and Maria Hando and their five children travelled even further. The Poor Board lost patience and decided that the burden on the poor rate must be relieved. It was an economy to pay for the assisted passage of the Handos and other impoverished Somerset families to Australia.

Thus seven Handos sailed with 814 migrants from Liverpool on 4 August 1852, hoping for a better life. Sadly, the elegant, re-fitted American clipper, the *Ticonderoga*, became a notorious fever ship. One hundred and eighty migrants died on the voyage or afterwards in quarantine, including William and Maria Hando and their two daughters, Anna Maria (16) and baby Emma. The three boys survived and landed at Melbourne on 22 December.

Eighteen-year-old Charles sought his fortune in the gold fields but his most precious discovery was Ruby Mansell from Tipperary. They had five children, all girls.

The young orphan brothers, Henry (10) and George (7), were adopted but kept their name. We cannot trace George, but Henry married Elizabeth Ellson and they had 11 children, including eight boys. The hundreds of Handos spread over Victoria, New South Wales and Queensland are all descended from an orphaned economic migrant from rural Somerset.

David Hando

The wrong packet

This story concerns three of my third cousins four times removed. On 6 October 1825, Martha Outhet, wife of Cloughton shoemaker, William Outhet, purchased some sulphur at a Scarborough druggist's shop. She intended to dose her children with brimstone and treacle in the mistaken belief that it would prevent them catching smallpox, then rife in Cloughton.

Having other business in town, she arranged to collect the sulphur on her way home. The packet of medicine was left on the counter for

her. During her absence another customer ordered an ounce of white arsenic which was also left on the counter for collection later. Martha returned and, unnoticed by anyone, took the packet of arsenic by mistake and set off home.

When they saw the poison had gone, the shop staff tried unsuccessfully to discover who had taken it. They assumed nobody would consume it, as the packet was clearly marked 'poison'.

Unfortunately, Martha could not read. Next evening she mixed the arsenic with treacle and gave a spoonful to each of her daughters, Jane, five, Elizabeth, three and a half, and Martha, two. She then took a larger dose herself, intending to pass on the benefit of the medicine to her baby, Thomas, in her breast milk.

Within a short time, Martha and the girls were suffering the agonies of acute arsenic poisoning. A doctor was summoned but to no avail. By next morning, all William Outhet's family, save his son, were dead. The inquest verdict was 'accidental death, occasioned by poison unconsciously and innocently administered and taken'.

John Watson

St Laurence's Church, Scalby (pronounced Scawby) near Scarborough, North Yorkshire, where Martha Outhet and her family were buried

The faithful dog

My three-times-great-uncle, Charles Gough, was born in Manchester in 1782, the son of Quaker parents. He was a competent artist and a number of his paintings have survived.

In April 1805 he set off with his dog from an inn in Patterdale to climb Helvellyn. He was never seen alive again. He had fallen from Striden Edge, near Red Tarn on Helvellyn, and his remains were found three months later. His dog was still alive and had whelped a pup. Charles was buried in the Quaker burial ground at Tirrell near Keswick.

The story was immortalised by Sir Walter Scott in his poem 'Helvellyn', published in 1806. This was followed a year later by the

'Callander' by Charles Gough (© Wordsworth Trust).

'Beddgelert' by Charles Gough (© Wordsworth Trust).

poem 'Fidelity' by Wordsworth. A number of artists made paintings of the scene, the most famous one being *Attachment* by Sir Edmund Landseer, which is now in the St Louis Arts Museum.

Canon Rawnsley built a memorial to the memory of Charles on Helvellyn in 1891 and published a booklet, *Gough and his Dog.* Last year the Wordsworth Trust published another book about Charles Gough. A letter written by Charles to his brother Henry in 1805 has survived in the British Library.

As a beginner in genealogy it took me five years to prove my relationship to Charles. In the course of this I found a number of well-known people in my family tree, one of the most important being John Gough (1757–1825), the blind philosopher who taught John Dalton.

Peter Gough

War baby

My father, Phil, was captured at the fall of Singapore. As he was being transferred to work on the Death Railway in April 1942, my mother (who knew only that he was 'missing') was awaiting the birth of their first child. The details of the events surrounding the birth of this child are documented in an extensive diary that she kept at the time.

On 7 April my mother wrote:

'The past few weeks have been the worst in my life but I have done my utmost to have courage and believe that nothing worse has happened than that you are a prisoner of war ... our darling baby,

An extract from my mother Pat's diary (written in the form of letters to my father)

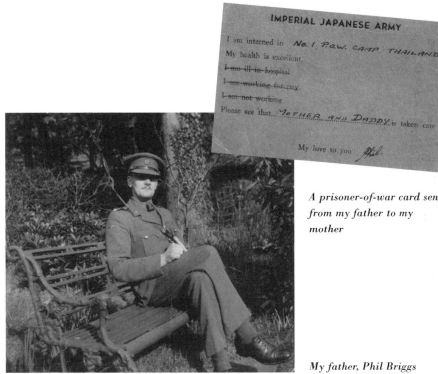

IMPERIAL JAPANESE ARMY

I am interned in *No. 1 P.O.W. CAMP, THAILAND.*

My health is excellent.

~~I am ill in hospital.~~

~~I am working for pay.~~

I am not working.

Please see that *MOTHER AND DADDY* is taken care

My love to you *Phil.*

A prisoner-of-war card sent from my father to my mother

My father, Phil Briggs

that we wanted so much, has given me so much to live for [and] in a few days now she should be here ... our Paddy will be born.'

But then on 18 April:

'Phil my sweet I hardly know how to bring myself to write the next few lines. Oh Phil, our baby girl was born at 7.40 p.m. yesterday. But ... there is some malformation of the spine and even should she live she may be a cripple for life ... Oh Phil to look at Paddy, she is the sweetest baby. She has deep set eyes and a chin like yours and her ears are just like yours too ... I am quite fit myself and I can have another baby when you come home.'

I was destined to be that baby. My elder sister died ten days after her birth.

Patrick Briggs

A poignant record

'21 January 1888 half past three.'

That's all it said. Written in a shaky hand in pencil on the flyleaf of the family bible, beneath the birth details of three children, the youngest of whom had died in infancy just a few months before.

I was intrigued. What could this date mean? It was obviously of some importance to the family, but there was no telling why.

It wasn't until a couple of years later on in my genealogy searches that I heard rumours that my husband's great-grandfather had drowned at sea. For generations the Seavill family had been hardy Bristol Channel sailing pilots and, later on, merchant shipping men. I began to wonder about that date in the bible again and started searching the death records of merchant seamen. And sure enough, there it was, reported in the local paper just a couple of days after the event: 'On the morning of 21st January 1888 the SS *Constance* ran

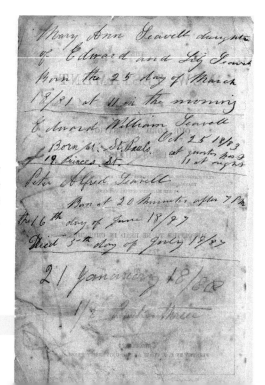

The family bible page showing Lily Seavill's faint inscription at the bottom of the page

onto rocks in dense fog off Plymouth Sound with the loss of three lives' – one of them was Quartermaster Edward Seavill, aged 29.

Those few words had been all Edward's grieving wife Lily could bring herself to write and, not long after, she reputedly took her own life. But this poignant record brought Lily back to life for me and I could imagine her pain and sorrow. It is human details like this which make family history research so fascinating to me.

Katherine Seavill

The Bristol Times and Mirror *report of the wreck of the* SS Constance, *dated 23 January 1888*

WRECK OF A BRISTOL STEAMER.

THREE LIVES LOST.

MIRACULOUS ESCAPES.

INTERVIEW WITH SURVIVORS.

[BY OUR OWN REPORTER.]

Early on Saturday a telegram was received at the offices of the Bristol Steam Navigation Company, Limited, giving information to the effect that the company's steamship Constance was wrecked off Plymouth that morning, in a dense fog, and three of the crew had been drowned.

About the same time the news reached the Commercial-rooms and the office of this newspaper, and the sad disaster became chief matter for conversation among the shipping community of the city.

In the course of the afternoon further details were ascertained by one of our staff, from which it appears that the Constance, which was one of the finest vessels of the fleet owned by the Steam Navigation Company, had become a total wreck, having broken her back.

The steamer left Bristol on Saturday, the 7th inst., with a general cargo. She called at Fowey, steamed thence to Plymouth, and from there to Antwerp. The outward voyage was accomplished in safety, and without any incident of an unusual character. Her cargo was duly discharged, and a fresh cargo of general merchandise shipped to the extent of 750 tons—her registered tonnage was about 560—and on Thursday morning last she left Antwerp for Plymouth. Fine weather was experienced up to noon on Friday, when a thick fog came on. The steamer proceeded slowly and cautiously, and just before midnight the Start Light was sighted very close in, the varying character of the fog—now thin now dense—allowing this. By the orders of the captain (H. F. Holt) the lead was thrown every few minutes, and all precautions seem to have been taken to avert disaster.

The steamer was proceeding slowly towards Plymouth Breakwater, and when within little more than a mile she suddenly struck a rock, and took a strong list over to starboard. There was deep water shown by the sounding, and the steamer had evidently got on to one of those rocks which rise sharply out of the water, the lead giving no indication of approach towards them. The captain, seeing how matters stood, and that the ship was filling rapidly, at once gave orders to launch the lifeboat and jolly boat, and this was done with all possible speed. The steamer rolled a good deal, and the sea was rough on the weather side, which rendered the launching of the boats a dangerous task. The mate, second mate, and three others were pitched to the leeward, and unhappily the three—Edward Seavill, quartermaster, William Wild, seaman, and Thomas Rees, fireman—were drowned. The chief mate and second mate caught, one hold of the rails, and the other a rope, and were by these means saved, the mate being dashed aboard again by a wave, and the second mate being, after some time, hauled on to the deck.

The captain and all hands were on deck when the steamer struck. All efforts to rescue the three men who were in the water were unavailing, and the rest of the crew—the steamer carried fifteen all told—got safely into the lifeboat and the jolly boat. They remained under the lee of the vessel, where there was comparatively smooth water, for some two or three hours waiting for daylight; but the wind from the south-west got a little stronger, and they were obliged to leave the Constance to her fate and look further to their own safety. The men in the jolly boat were transferred to the lifeboat, and they pulled for Plymouth, where they landed in safety. The jolly boat was allowed to go adrift. The shipwrecked mariners, who had lost all they possessed that they did not stand up in, then made their way, drenched to the skin by the heavy seas that had continually broken over them for the last four or five hours, to the local agent of the Steam Navigation Company. They do not speak in unstinted terms of

First aid for the miners

'Gravy Rings Around My Plate' is the life story of my great-uncle, Arthur Parfitt, and his life-long association with the St John Ambulance movement, as told by his son Lewis. Arthur's story begins in the Welsh valleys, where, following in his father's footsteps, he started work underground in 1916 at the tender age of 14. These were harsh times: there was much poverty and the struggle to survive in the mining communities was tough, especially in the 1920s and 1930s.

A letter of commendation received by Arthur for his praiseworthy action in a mining accident at Deep Duffryn

The St. John Ambulance Brigade

HEADQUARTERS—8, GROSVENOR CRESCENT, LONDON, S.W.1.

LETTER OF COMMENDATION

7th May, 1963.

      The Chief Commissioner for Wales has drawn my attention to an accident which occurred at the Deep Duffryn Colliery on the 11th March, 1963, when you rendered first aid to a man who had been struck by a tub which pinned him against the coal loading chute at the bottom of the pit.

      There is little doubt that your swift perception and knowledge were responsible for saving the life of this man and it gives me great pleasure, therefore, to send you this Letter of Commendation to place on record my appreciation of the excellent manner in which you dealt with this case. Your actions are indeed praiseworthy and in the best traditions of the St. John Ambulance Brigade.

Commissioner-in-Chief.

County Staff Officer (Cadets) (A) A. Parfitt,
Aberdare County,

Members of the St John Ambulance Brigade, Deep Duffryn Colliery, with Arthur Parfitt on the right

There were no medical facilities at mines in those days and when miners were hurt, sometimes in horrific accidents, they were rescued by fellow workers and taken home to the family. Arthur became interested in first aid and trained with St John Ambulance. Over the following years, he rescued miners from near-death situations. He played a big part in the miners' campaign for decent medical facilities at their pits – starting by begging the often reluctant owners for use of a basic shed as a first aid post.

Eventually, with mining reforms in 1947, a properly staffed medical centre was set up and later Arthur was made Medical Centre Attendant at Deep Duffryn Colliery. He received letters of commendation from the Priory for Wales, St John's Ambulance, for his efforts for the movement and for mining.

'Gravy Rings Around My Plate' is more than 40 pages long, beautifully written and richly deserving to be read. Copies are with the Miners' Museum, Port Talbot, and the St John Museum, London. The title refers to the fact that Arthur never managed to finish his dinner – it always had to be re-heated as he kept being called out to accidents!

Avril Vokes

'Run for your life!'

My grandfather, Alexander Mitchell, was born in Scotland in 1871. He went to live in London where he met a young married lady, Nora Caine. Soon after, Nora had a son, followed by a daughter. Some time around 1912 the young couple ran away to Ludlow where Alexander became a foreman at a chemical factory, the Hooley Hill Rubber and Chemical Company. After three more children, Nora was taken badly ill. The couple married in 1915 but Nora died in October. His daughter has told me how heartbroken Alexander was. By that time his eldest son was working at the factory with him.

> I consider they have given their lives for their country just as much as the soldier on the battlefield, and to the best of their strength and ability they did all that was possible to stem what they knew would be a great disaster.

From the Ashton-under-Lyne Reporter, 14 July 1917,
quoting the coroner, Mr. G. S. Lereeche.
Since I submitted the story to the Family History Project,
the Lord Lyon of Scotland has agreed to create a Grant of
Arms in memory of Alexander Mitchell. The motto will be
'Strength through Sacrifice'.

Further details of the explosion confirm the first reports that almost 50 people have lost their lives in the disaster. So far, 41 deaths have occurred, but it is stated that 15 people are still missing, though this number may include one or two children who have been given shelter by neighbours. On every hand there is nothing but praise for the heroic conduct of several workmen who, though they had every opportunity of reaching a place of safety before the explosion occurred, continued to do everything they could to extinguish the fire which was the first cause of the catastrophe. Gradually they were forced back, and were eventually blown to pieces. Two men who have given their lives in devotion to duty are Mr. H. S. Dreyfus and Mr. Alexander Mitchell, manager and foreman respectively. Both ran about the workshops giving the alarm and advising workpeople to seek safety until the last.

From The Times, *16 June 1917*

In 1917 the factory was making glycerine for ammunition to be used in the First World War. On 13 June, a fire broke out on the loading bay which quickly spread into the factory. Alexander told his 17-year-old son to 'run for your life'.

Alexander went back to help others get to safety. The fire reached the main area and the glycerine exploded. The explosion was recorded over 100 miles away.

Alexander's son was blown off his feet and woke 100 yards further up the road. The first thing he saw was the body of his father, which had been blown from the factory to fall in the same street.

An inquest was held and the incident was reported by the national papers. My grandfather was recognised as having given his life to save many others, but left five children orphaned.

Anthony Mitchell

Savaged by a bear

My four-times-great-grandmother, Mary Rodger, was killed by a bear kept for bear baiting in 1790, at High Green near Sheffield.

I stumbled across the information by pure accident when reading a diary someone had kept at the time detailing the day-to-day happenings of the village. This in turn led me to see if it was possible that it had been reported in the newspapers of the time. Luckily for me it had, and I now have a report of the incident written in the rather flamboyant style of the day.

The bear savaged her in her own home and her husband tried to save her. She died a very painful death two days later. This is before registration so it is unusual to be able to find out how an ancestor died at that time.

Lyn Howsam

A report on the attack on
Mary Rodger in the
Sheffield Register, 17
December 1790

SHEFFIELD, December 17.

A circumstance not less dreadful in its consequence, than disgraceful to a civilized nation, happened at High Green, a few miles from hence, on Saturday morning last. A *Bear* kept there by one Cooper, for the *amusement* of the country people at their *wakes*, got loose—pinched it is supposed of food—and entered the dwelling of a person named Rogers. The unfortunate wife of the man was sitting with one child on her lap, and another beside her, when the creature seized her with all the savage ferocity incident to its nature, and tore her in a manner too shocking to particularize. The cries of the poor unfortunate, and of the children, reached Rogers and the Bearward, who, almost at the same moment entered the house, and beheld a sight sufficient to appal the most callous mind—what then must have been the feelings of a husband?——He flew to the animal, but was unable to wrench its jaws from the object of its fury. Cooper then struck it on the head with a hammer, but the haft flying off, the blow was powerless; it however turned the bent of its rage on him, and it pursued him until he was nearly exhausted with fatigue, and he must have fallen a victim, had not the neighbours, alarmed at the outcries, come up with him, and, at a second shot, laid it dead.—The woman expired in dreadful agony on Monday. We hope and trust this dreadful and unparalleled accident will finally abolish, in these parts, that unchristian, barbarous species of diversion—*bear-baiting!*

Family Skeletons

One of the joys of family history is the journey into the unknown. Many people uncover surprising stories about their distant ancestors – and sometimes the results of more detailed investigations are quite shocking. The stories featured in this section highlight how an event that occurred centuries ago still echoes down the years, leaving rumours and whispers that can be used to spark your own investigation in archives.

Two particular examples spring to mind. The first piece of research began with vague talk in the family of a 'black sheep', who was 'bad blood'; but no one seemed to know any actual details of how this reputation had been earned. Research in the 1901 census revealed that the individual in question was languishing in prison. Further digging in the archives uncovered the reason why – he had tried to murder his mistress by cutting off her head!

The next case also began with a chance remark – 'they hanged him for it'. Exhaustive newspaper research uncovered the story of a relative who had murdered his wife in a crime of passion, and had been sentenced to hang. While awaiting execution, he was imprisoned in Reading gaol, where one of his fellow prisoners was Oscar Wilde. The author was so moved by the man's sorry tale that he was inspired to write 'The Ballad of Reading Gaol' about him.

Also featured in this section are stories about smuggling, including research into an ancestor who was executed for his part in a raid on a Customs House; a nineteenth century duel; bigamy; illegitimacy; and deportation. Of course, not all our ancestors were as badly behaved as these, but they certainly add some colour to the family tree!

Research Tips

Crime and criminality seem to be key themes reflected in these stories, and you can trace the outline of many court cases that were the result of our ancestors' more nefarious deeds. Trials of lesser offences took place at 'quarter sessions', and the records generated by these local courts are stored at county record offices. More serious offences were heard either at assize hearings by itinerant justices, or were referred to the central royal courts of justice. These records are largely held at the National Archives, where you will also find calendars of prisoners, transportation lists and petitions for clemency.

However, one of the best sources for trial reports – often featuring more descriptive accounts of proceedings – are local and national newspapers. It is also worth looking for contemporary pamphlets describing more notorious proceedings, again stored at either local level or at specialist institutions such as the British Library.

Smuggling often features in these criminal records, but it was also closely monitored by the customs and excise officers employed by the Crown to stamp out illicit activity. Letter books and papers of the various local Custom Boards, as well as replies from Customs House in London, can be found at the National Archives, and often provide a vivid account of smuggling.

Of course, not all family secrets feature violent acts but other topics traditionally 'swept under the carpet' – including illegitimacy and bigamy – which can also be researched through the records.

In Reading gaol by Reading town

When I was younger, I remember my grandmother talking with my mother and saying 'they hanged him for it'. I got the impression they were talking about a family member, but quickly forgot about it.

Many years later I decided to trace my family tree and, in the process, remembered the conversation and asked my mother about it. She did not know the details, but said she thought the man was a soldier, who had shot his wife, about the time of the Boer War. She said he was a relative.

WOOLDRIDGE THE CONDEMNED

This week we were informed that Wooldridge, who is under sentence of death, is bearing up wonderfully well under the circumstances. Since his conviction he has been frequently visited by the Chaplain of the prison (the Rev. M. T. Friend), to whose ministrations he listens with great attention. He takes daily exercise and seems in very good health. The execution has been fixed for next Tuesday.

Mr. R. S. Wood, Wycombe, has been working indefatigably to secure a reprieve for Wooldridge. The depositions taken at the trial have been forwarded to the Home Secretary, and a petition in favour of a commutation of the death sentence is in circulation and has been extensively signed by the officers and men of his regiment. Should this appeal be unsuccessful, special representations will be made to the Queen to exercise the royal clemency, not only on the ground that the tragedy was unpremeditated, but also that it occured in the precincts of the Royal borough.

The Rev. Arthur Robins, at Holy Trinity Church, on Sunday, told the congregation that a petition was in the vestry, and all who desired to sign it could do so.

A commutation of the sentence of death is prayed for on the following grounds :—

1.—That for a period of about ten years previously to the murder the condemned man had served as a trooper in the Royal Horse Guards.

2.—That up to within four weeks of the murder the condemned man and his wife (the deceased) had loved each other passionately and devotedly.

3.—That about four weeks before the murder, as shewn in the evidence, the deceased woman formed and nourished an unfortunate attachment with another man, and from that time she began to shew a dislike for her lawful husband and treated him with contempt and coldness, which culminated in the deceased woman drawing up and sending to her husband a document for him to sign to the effect that he would keep away and never have anything to do with her, although he loved her as passionately as ever.

4.—That the condemned man undoubtedly received terrible provocation at the hands of the wife whom he loved.

5.—That we believe that when the murder was committed he was, owing to the provocation received, in a state of frenzy and for the time being unaccountable for his actions.

6.—On account of his previous good character and on account of the aged father and other members of his family.

7.—And further your memorialists would urge the strong recommendation to mercy which accompanied the verdict of the Jury, and which recommendation was then and there at the Court committed to writing and signed by all the Jurymen.

Reports on the crime from the Windsor Chronicle, 3 *July 1896 and 7 July 1986*

I established that the best way to track down stories such as this was to check the historic references to crimes and trials in the indexes to *The Times* in the British Library Newspaper Library at Colindale in London. I only had the name – Charles Wooldridge, my great grandmother's brother – and rough date, but found the story and references to the *Windsor Chronicle* where the whole saga was reported over a few months from start to finish. The soldier, who was in the Horse Guards, had cut his wife's throat in a crime of passion as she had two-timed him. He was caught and sentenced to hang.

He was in Reading gaol in 1896, at the same time as Oscar Wilde, and was the subject of 'The Ballad of Reading Gaol', one of Wilde's most famous poems.

Alan Stubbs

The tea smuggler

My four-times-great-aunt, Hester Frohock, married Robert Hanning in 1733 in London. Two books on Folkestone describe how 'smuggler Robert Hanning testified [he] had sold brandy and tea to a value of £40,000 a year', and that 'Robert Hanning gave evidence to a Royal Commission in 1746'.

Walker is Inclined to beleive that Robert Hanning did no beat the said Watchman at all, because he had no Weapon in his hand, which he apprehends) wou'd do any Execution, but the said John Hanning, and Watson had both Loaded Whips, and the said Watson declaring that he had beat one of the Watchmen handsomely, and no other Watchman being beat as Walker heard, he beleives that the Watchman Died of the blows he received from Watson, and John Hanning.

22 July 1743.

George Walker

Section of the testimony of George Walker, one of Hanning's accomplices, which describes the murder of the watchman, Samuel Alexander. Two of the gang attacked him with whips when he interrupted a delivery of tea to a warehouse near Bunhill Row in London. (TNA: PRO SP 26/62)

In the 1746 *Journal of the House of Commons*, I found evidence from Mr Samuel Wilson, grocer. For the last three to four years Robert Hanning, he had been told, supplied the smugglers with tea, formerly at Dunkirk and, since the war with France, at Flushing. Hanning had been several times to England, where the tea was run into London and put into warehouses.

Hanning was formerly a smuggler who was indicted for murder and absconded. He was later pardoned, possibly on condition that he made 'certain discoveries' about smuggling. Some time before 1736, he gave Sir Robert Walpole a private account of what the receipts from smuggling might amount to. These were £1 million a year, of which £800,000 was for tea. Abraham Walter, a tea dealer and Hanning's brother-in-law, said Hanning and other tea dealers at Calais, Boulogne and Dunkirk knew what quantities were shipped at these ports.

Documents on Hanning in the National Archives consist of a petition by him of 1743 to the Commissioner of Customs, giving details of the murder of the watchman, Samuel Alexander, and requesting his pardon, and a letter from the Treasury Chambers a week later to the Lords Justices asking for mercy, as Hanning 'did not strike the said watchman, Samuel Alexander'.

George Watson, one of Hanning's associates, was executed for the murder.

Alvine Hill

Whisky galore

During the Second World War, the SS *Politician* sank in Ereskay.
Arnott and Young the ship-breakers, Dalmuir, Glasgow, were given the
job of salvaging the wreck. My grandfather, Robert Stewart, was the
foreman in charge of the job and my uncle, Robert Stewart Jnr, also
worked on it, as did my father, William Sweeney, as a diver's helper.

We have lived for years with the story of what happened on the
island – how everybody salvaged the whisky, using bales of silk cloth as
ropes and played cards with Jamaican 10-shilling notes. My aunt used
to tell us the men were playing cards one night when a knock came at

My grandfather Robert Stewart,
1879–1952

My father, William Sweeney (1921–84), with my mother Isabella (nee Stewart)

The Jamaican 10-shilling note.

the door – it was the excise men. They quickly threw away all the money onto the fire. She told us how people hid the whisky in the thatch of their cottages and one woman passed the excise man with a pram full of whisky with the baby on top! This whole incident was made into a film called *Whisky Galore*.

My younger brother, Robert Stewart Sweeney, was born during this time in Ereskay. Several members of my family have made trips back to Ereskay and to their amazement, some of the older people remembered my family 50 years later! My aunt Molly is the only one still alive and she gives a vivid account of Ereskay, with lots of documentation about her time there.

William Sweeney

A double life

Like all genealogists I eagerly awaited the online 1901 census. I had already checked the microfiche and found my great-grandmother, Phoebe Ann Cropper, in West Bromwich, along with her children. But where was great-grandfather, Thomas Cropper? When the census was finally up and running I found him – in Stafford gaol!

Further research in Stafford Record Office and the local newspapers revealed that he had been convicted in 1900 of bigamy and sentenced to 15 months' hard labour. I had suspected this for some time, but now I had the proof.

Thomas married Sarah Jane Mills in 1867 and they had four children. Sarah and her children were in Middlesbrough in the 1881 census, but Thomas was in West Bromwich, shown as a single man.

(Printed by authority of the Registrar General)				CERTIFIED COPY of an ENTRY OF MARRIAGE Pursuant to the Marriage Act 1949			TG 5252

Registration District DUDLEY

1867. Marriage solemnized at Parish Church in the District of Tipton in the County of Stafford

Columns:— 1	2	3	4	5	6	7	8
No.	When married	Name and surname	Age	Condition	Rank or profession	Residence at the time of marriage	Father's name and surname	Rank or profession of father
248	September 15 1867	Thomas Cropper	21	Bachelor	Labourer	Tipton	Thomas Cropper	Labourer
		Sarah Jane Mills	19	Spinster	—	Tipton	Jonas Mills	Puddler

Married in the Parish Church according to the Rites and Ceremonies of the Established Church by after Banns by me. Wm Ker

This marriage was solemnized between us,	Thomas Cropper X his mark	in the presence of us,	Daniel Bennett
	Sarah Jane Mills X her mark		Emma Davies X her mark

Certified to be a true copy of an entry in a register in my custody, Registrar Superintendent Registrar } JP Shaleum

CAUTION.—It is an offence to falsify a certificate or to make or knowingly use a false certificate or a copy of a false certificate intending it to be accepted as genuine to the prejudice of any person or to possess a certificate knowing it to be false without lawful authority.
WARNING: THIS CERTIFICATE IS NOT EVIDENCE OF THE IDENTITY OF THE PERSON PRESENTING IT

Date 20th March 2002

Certificates recording Thomas Cropper's marriage to Sarah in 1867 and his subsequent bigamous marriage to Phoebe in 1882

1882. Marriage solemnized at *Parish church* in the *Parish* of *Netherton* in the County of *Worcester*.

No.	When Married.	Name and Surname.	Age.	Condition.	Rank or Profession.	Residence at the time of Marriage.	Father's Name and Surname.	Rank or Profession of Father.
442	Jan 28 1882	Thomas Cooper	36	Bachelor	Labourer	West Bromwich		deceased
		Phoebe Ann Hill	22	Spinster		West Bromwich	Edward Hill	Iron roller

Married in the *Parish church* according to the Rites and Ceremonies of the Established Church, by — or after Banns by me.

This Marriage was solemnized between us, Thomas Cooper / Phoebe Ann x Hill — in the Presence of us, Edward Hill / Sarah Maria x Hill   A. J. Marriott Vicar

CERTIFIED to be a true copy of an entry in the certified copy of a register of Marriages in the Registration District of *Dudley*
Given at the GENERAL REGISTER OFFICE, under the Seal of the said Office, the 23rd day of March 19 98

MXA 222654

Then Thomas married Phoebe Ann Hill in 1882 at Netherton and they had 13 children. I checked the divorce records but found nothing.

The newspaper reports state that Sarah Jane said he was a cruel man, but Phoebe Ann pleaded for clemency as she said Thomas had always been kind to her and her children. Was one of the 'wives' lying? Or had Thomas become a changed man with Phoebe? And how had he been found out? No clue as to that one yet!

When people first learn you are a genealogist they usually ask if you have found any skeletons in the closet. Imagine their reaction when you can truthfully say, 'Well, my great-grandfather was a convicted bigamist!'

Jeffrey Best

Black sheep

From an early age, snippets of information reached me about my great-grandfather, Thomas Makens (1848–1925). Grandma said he was 'lively'. Father said he was a 'black sheep' and mum muttered darkly about 'bad blood'.

I grew older and asked questions. He had wasted his inheritance, said grandma, drunk solidly for seven years! He went to prison for attempted murder, said father. When, how, why – I kept asking. Nobody seemed to know.

It was not until 2002, while looking through the 1901 census, that the words 'husband in prison' jumped out from my great-grandmother's entry. I searched newspapers for 1901 for any reports and amazingly the first reel of film revealed all.

It seems that Thomas had a mistress, Emeline Smith, a pub landlady near his house, whom he believed was unfaithful. She insulted him so badly that Thomas really lost it and decided to cut off her head, and then his own! He twisted a towel and then a length of rope around her neck. A terrible struggle ensued and half the street helped rescue Mrs Smith. Incredibly she refused at first to bring charges, and Thomas was not arrested until next day.

In court Thomas conducted his own defence. The newspaper reports are full of blanks to disguise his rough language! The judge seemed almost sympathetic and Thomas was found not guilty of attempted murder, but guilty of attempting grievous bodily harm. He was given 18 months' hard labour.

All this took place in the street where I grew up, less than a mile from my present home. I pass through the scene of Thomas's crime almost every day.

Jill Wright

STOWMARKET ASSAULT CASE

Thomas Makens (54), drover, was indicted for attempting to strangle Emeline Smith, with intent to kill and murder her, at Stowmarket, on March 14th. Mr. Stewart prosecuted, and prisoner pleaded not guilty. – Mrs. Emeline Smith said her husband kept the Vulcan Arms in Bury Street, Stowmarket. On March 14th prisoner visited the house and asked for a half a pint of beer. There was no one else in the house with the exception of a little girl, and prisoner went to her room and said he was going to do what he liked with her. She tried to get away, and he swore to cut her head off. He got a towel off the roller and pulled it tight round her neck. She called for help, but he kept the towel in that position for some minutes. He next flung her on to the floor, and, taking a rope out of his pocket, he put the noose part of it round her neck and pulled it tight. She got into the next room and managed to struggle into the street, with the prisoner still pulling. A Mrs. Beaumont, who saw her, pushed prisoner back into the room, and the door was closed. A young man then came with a knife and cut the rope, when she was very nearly done for. Prisoner alleged that prosecutrix told him he ought to be led about with a halter like the horses on the market, and he said, "I've got a halter for you," producing the string from his pocket. He chased her round the room, and she caught her foot in a hole in the carpet and fell, and he fell on top of her. He then got the rope over her neck, and he told her the more she pulled the tighter it would get. When he found her going for the street he commenced to pull. – Prisoner asked witness if he had not had intercourse with her on frequent occasions, but she denied it. She, however, admitted having accompanied him to two public houses. – His lordship told prisoner that assuming these immoral relations to have been true, it did not give him the right to put the rope round her neck.

Suffolk Advertiser *report on the Makens case as heard at the Suffolk Assizes, 8 June 1901*

The most notorious murder in Sussex

I first came across Benjamin Tapner at the Waterfront Museum, Poole, while on holiday. I entered the Smuggler's Den and listened to a true story of the raid on the Poole Custom House.

I knew I had Tapners in my family history but had done no research on them. I spoke to a museum assistant who arranged for me to visit the archivist the next day, and was shown a book, supposedly written by the Duke of Richmond, which I read.

I mentioned Benjamin to my mother who confirmed the story was true and that there was a stone in Chichester commemorating it. An uncle had shown it to her and was very ashamed of it.

Benjamin Tapner was hanged in 1749 for the murder of Daniel Chater, which was described as the most notorious murder in Sussex. The incident began with a raid on the Customs House at Poole to recover contraband and it led to the torture and murder of two men.

The smugglers break open the Custom House at Poole (right). The two Custom House officers, William Galley and Daniel Chater, are whipped by the smugglers (opposite). This culminated in the murder of Galley and Chater: Galley was buried alive, and Chater thrown into a well. For this crime Benjamin Tapner, William Carter, John Cobby, John Hammond, and Richard Mills the elder and younger were hanged. William Jackson escaped this fate by dying a few hours after the death sentence was pronounced.

The outrage at the time led to huge rewards for information and the case led to the break up of the notorious Hawkhurst Gang and the reduction of the 140% tax on tea.

There is a lot of information about the case and several museums refer to it. I have followed up many minute leads and continue to locate more details, as I have a personal interest: Benjamin was my five-times-great-uncle.

Janette Scarborough

The last 'witch'

The last witch hunt in England took place at Wilstone, near Tring in Hertfordshire, in 1751. My family, the Gregorys, lived at Wilstone at that time and I still farm some land in the village.

An old woman, Ruth Osborn, was accused of putting a curse on one John Butterfield. The town criers of Hemel Hempstead, Leighton Buzzard and Winslow announced that a ducking was to take place on the 22 April. That day a huge crowd converged on Tring where the 'witch' had taken refuge in the church and they threatened to burn down the town unless Ruth Osborn and her husband were handed over.

The old couple were dragged two miles to Wilstone, ducked in the pond and Ruth was drowned. Her body was laid out in an upstairs room at the Half Moon, which is still a pub in the village, and three

The Half Moon public house at Wilstone where the 'witch's' body was laid out in an upstairs room and the coroner's inquest was conducted

days later a coroner's inquest was conducted there. I have a copy of that inquest and one of the people who gave evidence was my ancestor, Robert Gregory, a yeoman and chief constable, who had unsuccessfully attempted to stop the ducking. His house still stands in Wilstone.

Thomas Colley of Tring, one of the ringleaders, was tried for murder and hanged at a crossroads half a mile away, where his body hung in chains from the gibbet for several years.

I have many documents about the event and have constructed a family tree of more than 400 Gregorys going back to 1250 in the area.

Ivor Gregory

Extract from the inquest testimony of Robert Gregory

This Examinant on his oath says that he lives at Wilston Green in the Parish of Tring aforesaid and about 2 or 3 of the clock in the afternoon of Monday the 22nd Day of April last some of his children came in to this examinants house and said they have got them, which this examinant understood to be John Osborn and Ruth his wife whom he had heard were to be duck'd on that Day as a Wizard and Witch. Upon that he went into one of his own fields called Day's field to find out whether the Alarm was true or not and there he saw a great number of people going towards some water in a Meadow called Ten acres, where he imagined they were going to duck the said poor people. That the said water being a running water some people had stop'd the current in order to pen a head for ducking them as Witches but this Examinant broke down the shank and told the mob that there was no water there whereupon several of them offered to strike at him with sticks and he believes they would, had he not gone away from them. And he further says that the number of people there assembled might be near 4000 but says that he does not know anyone of them and that they were all strangers to him.

A mother's crimes

A Liverpool ship was taking human charges into forced labour on Jamaica's plantations as early as 1698. My seven-times-great-grand-stepmother was one of 12 petty criminals sent there from the Isle of Man aboard the *Speedwell*, commanded by Peter Travers. She was Christian Hampton, owner of Ballabunt Farm, where our family have lived for four centuries.

Christian was convicted of stealing two lambs, despite having plenty of sheep of her own. The first trial in 1696 is perfectly recorded; found guilty, she was released pending sentence. But before she returned to court, Christian stole another lamb and was sentenced to death. She joined 11 others awaiting execution, some convicted, for example, of stealing cheese. They languished in the dungeon of Castle Rushen and there Christian gave birth to a son, Nicholas, my seven-times-great-uncle.

In January 1698, Lord Derby offered the 12 mercy of life – transportation to Jamaica's sugar plantations – which they accepted. After boarding the *Speedwell* they were never heard of again. Proof exists that they were weak from brutal imprisonment and all probably died at sea because the *Speedwell* arrived in Kingston safely.

Before embarking, Christian had her baby 'taken from its mother's breast by force'. The tough youngster was taken home by his father, Christopher, who was uniquely given liberty to marry an additional wife for the sake of the child. A bachelor, Nicholas lived happily with his younger half-brother, to whom he had to relinquish his inheritance of Ballabunt due to his mother's crimes.

Hampton Creer

The oath of abjuration which sent the 12 prisoners to the Jamaican plantations
(Manx National Heritage)

A crime of passion

My eleven-times-great-uncle, Nicholas Glanvill, a wealthy merchant of Tavistock, and his daughter Eulalia were at the centre of a notorious crime of passion in late sixteenth-century Plymouth.

Eulalia loved a local young man of low status, and Nicholas arranged instead for her to marry an elderly miser, William 'the Wealthy' Page. To cut a long and well-recorded story short, Eulalia married Page, but plotted with her lover and some servants to kill her husband. The crime was immediately uncovered, the perpetrators charged (I have full details of the crime), and they were eventually sentenced to death

Sir John Glanvill (1542–1600), Judge of the Common Pleas (courtesy of Lincoln's Inn). This portrait of Sir John in his judge's robes still hangs in Lincoln's Inn, where he was trained as a barrister from 1567. He became a judge in 1598 (after the trial of his niece Eulalia) and died in a fall from his horse while on circuit two years later.

Kilworthy manor, near Tavistock, Devon, seen here in an engraving from the 1800s, was built in the 16th century and became Sir John Glanvill's family home. The house still stands, a little modernised, and is now a residential centre for children with learning disabilities. It is said to be haunted by Sir John and, more usually, his niece Eulalia Page.

in Barnstaple (plague prevented the trial being staged elsewhere).

The case captured people's imaginations and Eulalia's story became the subject of many ballads. Sir Francis Drake interrogated Eulalia and her accomplices in Plymouth. It is even said that Nicholas's celebrated brother (my ten-times-great-grandfather), Sir John, was the presiding judge. In fact, the records state the judge was a justice Anderson, though her uncle John was probably Eulalia's lawyer. Eulalia escaped the burning her accomplices suffered but was hanged.

Eulalia's wailing ghost is still said to haunt Kilworthy, Sir John's manor house in Tavistock, a still-beautiful place I was delighted to visit a few years ago. I am John's direct descendant, and there are many other interesting stories to tell about my ancestors.

Rick Glanvill

Scotland's penultimate duel

In 1783 William Gurley, my relative, was born on his father's sugar plantation in St Vincent, West Indies. He attended Eton from 1796 to 1769. He married Elizabeth Marsh of Ford, Northumberland, in 1812 in Berwick-upon-Tweed and they had seven children.

In October 1824, while residing temporarily in Pitt Street, Edinburgh, Gurley got into a fight at the Black Bull inn with J. B. Waistell, a London lace merchant's representative, over money due to him from a bet at the St Leger that September. Waistell refused to pay, negotiations failed and a duel was arranged for 30 October at Salisbury Craigs near Arthur's Seat, Edinburgh.

This plan was aborted after policemen were seen 'dogging' the group and Gurley, Waistell, two doctors, two seconds and supporters decided instead to cross the Forth River to a secluded place near North Queensferry. Later in court John Duguid, an army friend and Gurley's second, claimed Waistell's pistol discharged before the count of 'three' – and Gurley fell without firing. Immediately Waistell was advised to

Miniature of William Gurley as a child

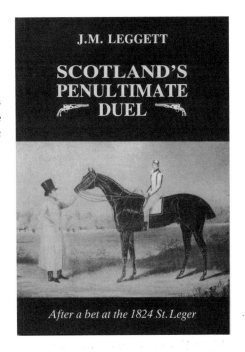

The cover of my book, Scotland's Penultimate Duel, *which describes the incident*

J.M. LEGGETT

SCOTLAND'S PENULTIMATE DUEL

After a bet at the 1824 St. Leger

'make the best of your way'. He took off, asking his friends to 'write to my father' (a clergyman in Cleasby). He was never caught.

Gurley's body was taken to the Mitchell's Inn (now Albert Hotel) where his widow stayed for a considerable time in 'the utmost agony of grief'. She moved with her children to Scarborough where an eighth child was born and baptised in April 1825. Mrs Gurley received an army pension till her death in Bawtry, Yorkshire, in 1862.

Joan Leggett

A wrong 'un

Having been told by a relative that my great-great-grandfather's second wife died in suspicious circumstances, I sent for the death certificate. The cause of death was 'had her throat cut by her husband, Thomas Emmett'. I knew Thomas was a butcher, so he had the tools! I was expecting to find a trial and execution, because the death certificate was so unambiguous, but the truth was even more gruesome.

A trip to Calderdale Library revealed a wealth of detail about the murder, the events leading up to it and the characters of the protagonists. He was a 'wrong 'un'. After driving my great-great-grandmother, Sarah Hoyle, to an early grave, he immediately set his cap at all eligible local females. They knew his reputation and rejected him.

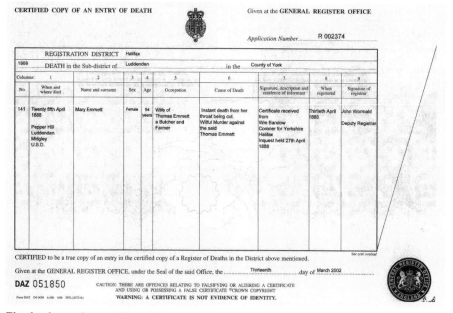

The death certificate of Mary Emmett

MURDER & SUICIDE
AT LUDDENDEN.

HORRIBLE TRAGEDY.

A BUTCHER PLAYS TERRIBLE HAVOC WITH HIS KNIFE.

STORY OF THE MURDERER'S LIFE.

FULL DETAILS.

The inhabitants of the quiet villages of Luddenden, Midgley and Luddenden Foot received a terrible shock on Wednesday forenoon last, when it became known that " murder most foul," followed by the suicide of the murderer, had been perpetrated in their midst. At first, the news was hardly credited, but it has been well said that "murder, though it hath no tongue, will speak with most miraculous organ," and it was not long before the details of the horrible tragedy were in the mouth and ears of everybody for miles around. Thomas Emmett, the man who was guilty of the frightful deed, carried on business as a butcher and small farmer at a place called Pepper-hill, situated a short distance from Luddenden Church, on the road leading to Midgley, and his victim was his own wife, with whom he resided alone, and whose head he all but severed from its body with his professional butcher's knife. The unhappy couple who have come to such an awfully tragic end were married some eighteen months ago. The man was 63 years of age at the time of his death, and his wife, Mary Emmett, was aged 53. They had both been married before, and each had grown-up children, who, however, did not reside with them.

He then went to Blackpool posing as a wealthy Yorkshire landowner, met Mary Thomas, wooed her and was accepted. All was well for a few months. Then he became obsessively jealous and accused her of being unfaithful. She left him once and then returned. He killed her one washday, then cut his own throat. The sight in the bedroom must have been terrible. The local bobby refused to go upstairs and sent a 16-year-old boy instead!

There is much more to discover about Mary. She was previously married and two of her children were born abroad (Ceylon and Newfoundland).

Is there a 'murder gene'? Thomas's grandson was hanged for murder just after the Second World War. My husband is a worried man!

Kathleen Gaukroger

The sheikh of Liverpool

I always thought my father's side of the family must have an interesting history because of their unusual surname, Quilliam, and I was right! I had just enrolled on a family history course when my husband called me to see an item on television about Abdullah Quilliam, who in 1856 was involved in some infamous murder trials for the defence.

He travelled widely, especially in North Africa, and in 1887 converted to Islam and became known as Sheikh Abdullah. He used to ride through the streets of Liverpool on a white horse in his robes and kept crocodiles and monkeys in his garden. He had two wives simultaneously, living in separate houses in the neighbourhood, and four children with each!

In 1908, Abdullah mysteriously disappeared, I think to Persia to fight for the Shah. The Shah lavished jewels on him, which one of his sons allegedly later gambled away in the south of France casinos.

He returned a few years later, under the name Professor Henry Marcel Leon, living in Bloomsbury, London, and taking the surname of his current mistress. On his death in 1932, she was disinherited and razed his properties to the ground, although his castle on the Isle of Man still stands today. He is buried in the Muslim section of the Brookwood Cemetery, Surrey.

I traced Abdullah's granddaughter, Pat Gordon, who is in her eighties; she has wonderful memories of him. Abdullah was my third cousin twice removed, but despite the distant relationship there is a definite physical resemblance between us, although I have no beard!

Linda Sutton

Plaque at Brougham Terrace, Liverpool, the first mosque in the UK, which was established by Sheik Abdullah Quilliam in 1887

Spirited away

My great-grandfather, James Kirkness, a cabinetmaker in Kirkwall, Orkney, branched out into the family grocers and Italian warehousing business in 1859. He became an agent for James Gilbey's wines and spirits. In 1875 he attempted to boost his profits by acquiring some smuggled geneva and rum from Captain Askam, an English sea captain who lived in Kirkwall. (Askam also had a mistress and family in the Faroe Islands.)

James Kirkness's shop in Kirkwall, Orkney, c. 1900. James' son John is the man on the right.

Kirkness and some other local businessmen were caught, charged, found guilty and fined (in Kirkness's case, £125 after appeal). Kirkness also lost his spirits licence, but for some reason retained his wine and beer licence.

The business survived and stayed in the family, trading as licensed grocers until 1981. The property is still owned by the family.

I have the original statements from the trial confirming the details of how the barrels were transported across the islands (by boat, horse and cart, and barrow). I also have an oak stave from one of the barrels which was found hidden in the rafters of the shop.

I also made contact with Captain Askam's great-grandson who lives in the Faroe Islands and have some additional information from him.

Bruce Gorie

Off to Gretna Green

James Lloyd, born in 1780, was the only son of Colonel Edward Lloyd. Aged 20, James eloped to Gretna Green with Joyce Williams, six years older than him and the oldest of 18 children. This was not the bride his parents had envisaged for their only son, who was heir to a large estate. The Colonel thundered north in pursuit but was too late to stop the marriage, which took place on 10 May 1801.

James joined the Hussars and was injured in the Peninsular Wars. He was captured by the French but exchanged for a French prisoner in June 1813, with the cartel of exchange signed by Wellington.

Colonel Lloyd, his father, died on 11 July 1818 and a family diary relates that 'the will declared the one son to be illegitimate, in what way no one knew. In consequence of this £4,000 a year went to another branch of the family.' I have since obtained a copy of the will which says, 'before I proceed to the disposition of my property it is necessary I acknowledge that I am not married to my dearly beloved Ann Baughan ... for more than 30 years acknowledged as my wife ... bitterly lament with the poignant anguish ... the stigma of illegitimacy of my beloved son'.

No wonder he was upset by his son's unconventional marriage at Gretna!

Susan Martineau

Cartel of Exchange.

Between Captain Lloyd of the 10.th Royal Hussars taken Prisoner on the 2.nd of June 1813 near Morales, and Captain Vernier of the 2.nd Regiment of French Dragoons taken Prisoner on the same day at Castromuño

Captain Lloyd having been permitted by the Enemy to return to the British Army, for the purpose of effecting his Exchange, Captain Vernier is sent to the French Outposts in Exchange for him and Captain Lloyd is released from his Parole from the Date hereof.

Given under my Hand and Seal at the Head Quarters of the British Army this fifth day of June 1813.

The cartel of exchange for James Lloyd

Soldiers and Heroes

Throughout history, Britain's armed forces have produced men and women of incredible valour, courage and bravery. Their actions are sometimes difficult to comprehend from our vantage point at the start of the twenty-first century. No one under the age of 60 knows what it was like to live under constant fear of aerial bombardment and invasion from the continent, while the horrors of the killing fields of France and Flanders during the First World War are but a distant memory. Therefore it is particularly important that we chronicle the experiences of our ancestors throughout these conflicts, from both a civilian and military perspective, lest we forget the sacrifices they made and the reasons why people were prepared to lay down their lives for us.

This collection of stories reflects the experience of ordinary people living through extraordinary times, where the difference between life and death was often decided by chance. Some accounts are astonishing, as demonstrated by the enterprising way in which a detainee at the Dachau concentration camp made his escape to Italy. Contributors have found family links with soldiers who were present at famous historical engagements, such as the Charge of the Light Brigade and the Battle of Waterloo, and detailed research has unearthed an eyewitness to Custer's last stand.

Other stories reflect the impact that conflicts have had on families left behind; the feelings of loss, tinged with pride, experienced by the family of a posthumous Victoria Cross recipient is particularly poignant. In contrast, there is a heart-warming story of a lady who tracked down her long-lost GI father in the USA.

Research Tips

As several of our contributors have discovered, there are a number of ways you can follow up stories that you have heard about your military ancestors. Photographs, badges or medals can often provide clues about which of the armed forces they were in, along with details of rank and unit (for example regiment or squadron). Once you have this information, try looking for a regimental museum or contact organisation; this is where you are likely to uncover context about the campaigns in which your relative fought and the places they visited during their military career.

Service records before 1923 are in the National Archives, along with operational records – including regimental war diaries from both world wars. Some information on gallantry medals can be gleaned from the files, although the citations for some awards are harder to track down. Many other aspects of war are covered, including a wealth of information relating to civil defence, rationing, evacuation, the Home Guard and the Blitz during the Second World War.

Your research list should include trips to the Imperial War Museum and the National Army Museum, where your research on an individual can be placed in a far wider context, including an insight into the development of uniforms, kit and weaponry. Finally, the Commonwealth War Graves Commission is an important organisation if you want to track down the whereabouts of a Commonwealth soldier buried overseas.

Custer's last stand

I started to research our families' histories for the benefit of my grandchildren. On my maternal grandmother's family, Pig(g)ford, I hit a block because the name did not appear to go back before the early eighteenth century. However through research and good luck I was able to prove a name change from Pigg. Although I had birth and marriage details for my three-times-great-grandparent I could find no death or burial details even though I found them relating to other members of the family. The previous generations were coal miners or agricultural workers who lived in Co. Durham or Northumberland.

Eventually I found that the family had emigrated to Pennsylvania, USA, in 1864 although one of their sons, Robert Piggford, had emigrated in the early 1850s. Robert married in Pennsylvania and his first son, Edward, was born in Elizabeth, Allegheny county, Pennsylvania, in 1856.

I found that Edward was in the Seventh Cavalry in 1876 and was

Edward Pigford c.1932 (Little Bighorn Battlefield National Monument)

Edward Pigford's death certificate. The date of birth is as he claimed when he enlisted, to make himself appear older – the correct date is in fact 1856.

under Custer's command. At the battle of the Little Big Horn he was in M Troop, part of Major Reno's group, which attacked the Indian village first. When Custer started his attack, Reno's group were able to withdraw. Edward was wounded twice but he survived, and he is reported to have witnessed Custer's last stand. He was later discharged for enlisting under age, and he went back to Pennsylvania where he resumed his life as a coal miner. He died in 1932.

Wilfred Laidler

One of the six hundred

I recently started researching my family history as a present for my daughter's 21st birthday. I had childhood memories of my grandfather to go on and little else, but managed to find his parents with the help of on-line resources and census records. When I found the address of my great-great-grandparents in 1881 I saw that they lived only a few doors away from the parish church in Sandhurst, Berkshire. I contacted the church offices who confirmed their indexes showed a family grave.

My great-great-grandfather, Edward Blissett c. 1858, immediately after his return from the Crimea

When I arrived to see for myself, I was thrilled to find a record of my great-great-grandfather's regiment on his headstone and also the notation that he was 'one of the six hundred' who fought in the Charge of the Light Brigade during the Crimean War and survived. At the National Archives, I was able to find copies of his full military history. I also contacted an on-line group of specialists, the Crimea War Society, who were extremely knowledgeable and supplied me with his full biography, including floggings and courts martial!

Sharing the information I'd found with other family members produced photographs out of dusty attics from as early as 1858.

Edward Blissett as an elderly man, sporting his medals which include the Crimea Medal with three clasps for the battles at Balaclava, Sebastapol and Inkerman, the Turkish Medal and the Long Service/Good Conduct medal.

They showed him in military uniform, sporting medals and clasps from Sebastapol, Inkerman and Balaclava. Now I had a complete picture of the person, and subsequently, as I've stood by his grave, I've reflected on how he endured carnage but returned home against all odds to marry and sire sons – who sired sons who sired sons who sired me!

Julie Noble

Resistance hero

I would like to write to you about my nan's uncle, William Sharp. He was a Dover-born man who fought through the First World War, serving at Ypres, where he lost his brother.

After the war he was in charge of one of the barges that brought supplies of war surplus goods back to Richborough. On one of the trips, he met his future wife, Germaine. They settled in Dover, then later in Calais. He became a naturalised Frenchman.

He ran a café in Calais which the Germans bombed in the Second World War and he later joined the French Resistance. The Gestapo captured him and tortured him for information, but he remained silent. Eventually they shot him in the street. The town of Calais has named a street after him, La Rue William Sharpe.

I would like to know more about this man but I only have half a newspaper clipping. I think his story deserves more study and recognition.

Darren Lench

*1960s article on William
Sharp from* The Dover
Express, *courtesy of my
grandmother, Vera Cannon,
who supplied many of the
details for my story*

DOVER MAN WILL ALWAYS BE HONOURED

n La Rue William Sharp

By Terry Sutton

William Sharp, in his army days.

A DOVER-BORN MAN who became a Frenchman and died at the hands of the Gestapo, has been honoured in the town of Calais. The municipal authorities in Calais have just named a new road after he hero—William Sharp, son of a Dover Harbour Board tug mate. William Sharp, who was to become a Resistance leader, was born in Chapel Lane, in Dover, in 1893. His father, Albert Edward Sharp, had big family of whom two sons and two daughters are alive today.

William Sharp, who moved to Albany Place with the family. went to St. Mary's School.

He started work as an apprentice pastry cook with Igglesden and Graves, Market Square caterers. When he was seventeen he joined the army and served with the 4th Battalion The Rifle Brigade.

He was in India and then returned to Europe for the 1914-18 war. Many were the battles he fought ....he was at Ypres when the Germans first used gas ....and was at Ypres where his brother Edward Sidney Sharp fell in battle.

After the war William Sharp was in charge of one of the barges that plied between Richborough and Calais bringing home war surplus stores.

It was on one of these trips to Calais that he met Germaine Deslace—the girl who was to be his wife.

They moved to Dover where their first daughter, Doris, was born in 1921. Shortly after this the three returned to Calais to live and in 1... William Sharp became a naturalised Frenchman.

He ran a dock-side cafe at Calais —this was wrecked by Hitler's shells and bombs—and also worked in a factory.

Soon after the German troops swept through France and captured the port, William Sharp noticed massive works being carried out on the cliffs on the ...

at Loos-Lille.

William Sharp—the lad who sat sat in the corner of the classroom at St. Mary's—was tortured by the Gestapo in an effort to get him to give full details of the Resistance organisation in Calais.

He was beaten, his face kicked in ...but 50-year-old William Sharp remained silent. Almost unrecognisable, he was eventually dragged out into the street and shot.

But before the fatal shots rang out, William Sharp, with his comrades Pierre, Marcel, Henri and Alphonse, sang the song they loved so much—"La Marseillaise."

After the liberation, William Sharp's body was exhumed and taken to Calais—the town where he was a hero.

And, near to La Porte de Dunkerque, he was laid to rest with full military honours.

Now, not far from the cemetery where William Sharp is buried, they have a new road.. La rue William Sharp.

One of William Sharp's brothers is Mr. Frederick Sharp, of 172 Heathfield Avenue, another is Mr. Albert Sharpe, of 19 Dickson Rd. There are two sisters, Mrs. Emma King, of 126 Heathfield Avenue, and Mrs. Ema Reeves, of Bekesbourne.

Mr. Fred Sharp often visits his brother's family in Calais and the grandchildren come over from France for holidays in Dover.

It is just one more link in the bond of friendship between Dover and Calais.

Escape from Dachau

My grandad was an Italian partisan during the Second World War. While working in Mussolini's Milan hospital as a nurse he helped wounded partisans to escape execution through the underground tunnels of the hospital.

One day he was found out and jailed. In jail he grew a beard so that his mom would not see the bruises and cuts on his face when she came to visit. He was then deported by train to Dachau concentration camp in Germany.

There he realised that he had to look for a way out. Every night an S.S. truck drove into the camp, dropped off some soldiers and drove out empty in the morning. One early morning my grandad sneaked out of the barracks, got into the truck, removed one of the spare truck tyres from its case and hid in the case. Later a German guard came into the truck with a torch, had a quick look around and eventually drove out of Dachau with my grandad hidden in the back.

Once free he travelled through the snow till he reached Austria where he worked as a barber in another concentration camp. Although 'free' my grandad could not return to Italy because he didn't have papers to cross the frontier. Eventually he received news that Mussolini was gathering troops, so he went to a German military office were he got the necessary papers to cross the frontier.

Once in Italy he threw those passes away and returned home.

Giovanni Nacci

How the West was won

My story is about my ancestral cousin, Thomas Moonlight, born to a poor farming family in Forfarshire, Scotland, in 1833. He left for the USA at 13, and fought as a captain for the Union in the bloody American Civil War, including successful exploits at the Battles of Pea Ridge and Westport.

After the war he commanded the famous Fort Laramie, but had a reputation for both brutality and incompetence. One story is that he and his troop left the fort to hunt Indians and after an unsuccessful day camped for the night. They awoke the next day to find the Indians had stolen their horses and they faced a long, and no doubt embarrassing, walk back to the Fort.

During this time, he was also dispatched with a troop of soldiers to Dodge City to encounter one of the most colourful characters of the time – Wyatt Earp.

Life after the army would also bring him in touch with other famous characters. He entered politics and served in a number of posts, including governor of the Wyoming Territory. During his term as governor, Thomas pardoned a young man who was locked in gaol following a robbery. The town was Sundance, Wyoming, and the person the famous Sundance Kid. This was the only time he was caught.

After his life in politics, Thomas Moonlight was appointed as US Ambassador to Bolivia where he served for a number of years. Thomas retired to Kansas, to take up his ancestral job of farming. He died at Leavenworth in February 1899.

Gary Lawrie

In Flanders fields

My husband is a nephew of Private John Condon, the youngest soldier to be killed in the First World War. He was aged 13 years and 9 months when he was killed in Flanders. He had given his age as 18 when he joined the Royal Irish Regiment.

He ran away with his cousin for adventure, but we can only try and imagine the horrors he faced. He was killed on 24 May 1915 before his 14th birthday. We have a piece of the boot that he was wearing when

My husband John laying a wreath on his uncle's grave, with the Mayor of Belgium and colleagues

The British Military Cemetary at Poelcapple, where John Condon and 7,441 others are buried

he was killed, with his army number on it. We also have his medals, all his war papers, and the letter to the family which told them of his death.

My husband, who is now in his seventies, is named after this famous boy soldier. He has an older brother and a sister in their eighties, and they are the last of that family. A monument in Private Condon's honour will be built soon here in Waterford.

Sally Condon

Lost in the fighting

I knew my uncle, Sid Morris, was killed in 1942, but I was unaware that close relatives had also perished in the First World War. For many years I encouraged and enabled pupils to go to visit their great-great-grandfathers' and great-great-uncles' graves in Flanders and the Somme but only when I retired in 2001 did I realise my lost opportunities.

Left: *my uncle, Bombadier Sid Morris, who was killed in 1942*
Opposite: *my great uncle Tom Horton, who survived the Great War; his brothers William Horton (killed in action 1915) and Frank Horton (killed in action 1916), shown here with their sister Charlotte Hateley (nee Horton), my grandmother*

I discovered that one relative possessed a box of unsorted, unresearched family documents and photographs relating to my father's family. Most intriguing was a letter, dated 17 June 1917, to 'Sister' (my grandmother) in Walsall from 'Brother Tom' in Liverpool. Tom Horton described his exploits at High Wood on the Somme, enigmatically mentioning 'two brothers and a brother-in-law … lost in the fighting'. Walsall's three wartime newspapers identified my two great-uncles and my great-uncle by marriage and also QMS Charles Jones, DCM, MM (my father's cousin), also mentioned in the letter, who survived the Great War along with my great-uncle Tom.

Further research revealed that another great-uncle was killed in March 1917. The twist in this story is that the first child of the Morris family born after the death of mother's uncle Ernest, born in 1918, was registered Sidney Ernest, but was baptised Ernest Sidney. Uncle Sid was killed outside Tobruk in June 1942.

In July 2003 a school party used my research to locate the grave of the youngest of the four great-uncles in Serre Road Cemetery and paid our family respects, almost certainly for the first time in 86 years.

Patricia Andrews

Born to be a fireman

My grandad was William Bridgman, known as Billie. As a small girl I remember seeing his red and black baton hanging on the wall, a souvenir of the old days. Later on I heard tales of his life as a fireman. He was a carpenter by trade, but that's another story.

He wrote many letters to the local paper and they were very descriptive of his life. He was born in 1864 in the Engine House in Kettering where his father was caretaker. With other local lads they would spend up to eight hours a day in the 'bucket line' and earn 18 pence (old money).

Jubilee celebrations outside the Engine House, 1887

Fire fighters outside the Engine House, 1892

In those days there were no electric bells to call up the brigade, and if there was a fire Billie and his father would run round and 'knock up' the firemen with wooden batons. The horses which pulled the old manual fire engine were kept in the George Hotel stables. Having been born in the fire station, he joined the force at the age of 20 and served for 34 years.

In 1887, Queen Victoria's Jubilee, the brigade assembled to take part in the town procession. I have a photo taken outside the Engine House and one of my grandfather in uniform (incidentally he was the first one to try on the uniform). I also have his long service medal, a bell, a whistle and newspaper cuttings of his letters.

In 1926, the year of my birth, the old Engine House was demolished.

Dorothy Bradbury

Looking for my GI father

I have always known that I had an American GI father, even as early as the age of five.

One Sunday in June 2002, my husband and I visited the Burtonwood Heritage Centre, RAF Burtonwood, Warrington, Cheshire. There were lists of the units and all the personnel who had served at the base from 1943 to 1993. The period that we were looking at was 1951–2, and the name of Napoleon B. Rushing was the only one that fitted.

I rang international directories to see if he was listed in the phone book for Jasper, Florida. There was only one Rushing listed there, a Baron Rushing. I telephoned Baron Rushing, who just happened to be Napoleon's younger brother; he gave us his address and telephone number.

Napoleon Bonaparte Rushing

My father and I in 2003

I wrote to Napoleon B. Rushing and in my letter I put down everything that I knew of him as well as some photographs of him with my mother and one of myself. I posted the letter and then waited.

I telephoned and asked for Napoleon. When he came on the telephone his first words were 'I'm the man in the photograph'. This did it – I knew that I had finally found my father after nearly 50 years. We made arrangements to go over to see him in June 2003.

My father has now visited us and met the rest of his family.

Larraine Parker

An old Persia hand

This is about Dudley Redfern, born in 1882, whose family flourished
in nineteenth century London. In 1850 his grandfather was a
warehouseman but by 1885 his father had become a landed proprietor.
At 18 Dudley went into banking in Brighton. His family objected to
Elsie, the attractive daughter of a successful builder, and he moved to
a firm of London shipping agents.

OLD ELSTONIANS   CRICKET TEAM, 1911.

J. J. WOOTTON.   J. P. WHITE.   NORMAN THORP.   F. A. D. REDFERN.   J. D. TWINBERROW.
(Custos Rotulorum)
R. G. PRIDMORE.   H. R. RENNIE.   G. F. M. CAMROUX.   W. N. SCHOLES.   L. J. BUSH.
(Captain).
H. G. ROSE.   M. G. ENRIQUEZ.

Two contrasting images of Dudley Redfern's life: an Old Elstonians cricket team
photograph of 1911 (Dudley is in the back row, second from right)

A postcard from Persia showing the interior of the mosque at Kazmain

In 1904 they sent him to Persia, resulting in a stream of postcards to Elsie. In six years he became the senior agent, learnt Persian and Arabic, dealt with diplomats and tribesmen, and gathered intelligence in the volatile atmosphere of pre-First World War Persia. His photographs also suggest that he had a very good time!

In 1910 he returned to England to marry Elsie. In London he became an entrepreneur with a Swiss businessman who ran off with their money and turned out to be German! Dudley and his family returned to his in-laws and temporary bank work.

In November 1914 Dudley offered his services as an old Persia hand but the War Office wanted him vetted because of his crooked German partner. While they dithered he was called up, trained as a motorcyclist and went to Egypt with the Mesopotamian Expeditionary Force. MI5 finally approved him and he was attached to the South Persian Rifles, newly created to stabilise the area. Sent to Basra in March 1917, he died there in July and was buried in the military cemetery. A question mark remains over his activities at the time of his death.

Carol Cambers

Serving under the Iron Duke

My great-great-grandfather, James Robinson, enlisted in the 33rd Regiment of Foot (Duke of Wellington's Regiment) in 1812 at the age of 18. He served in England, Ireland, Holland, Belgium and France. He took part in the Battle of Waterloo in 1815. I have his 1818 demobilisation documents, two marriage certificates and family letters, some of which create a mystery. Copies of documents obtained via the National Archives create another mystery.

His only son was quarrying in New York State in the 1850s. I have a detailed letter to his parents. I have a drawing of his home in West Riding where he was living when he registered the birth of his daughter's illegitimate child, together with various certificates.

I have copies of birth, death and marriage certificates of many of his descendants to the present day.

Keith Robinson

Section of James Robinson's discharge papers from the 33rd Regiment of Foot, 6 November 1818, which provides information on army conduct and civilian occupation as well as a physical description.

_33rd_ Regt. of _Foot_

Whereof _Lieut Genl Sr J C Sherbrooke GCB_ is Colonel.

THESE ARE TO CERTIFY,

1st.
Certificate of Age and Enlistment.
THAT _Private James Robinson_ born in the Parish of _Halifax_ in or near the Town of _Halifax_ in the County of _York_ was enlisted for the aforesaid Regiment at _Cork_ in the County of _Cork_ on the _fifth_ Day of _June 1812_ at the Age of _Eighteen_ for _Limited Service_.

2nd.
Certificate of Service.
THAT he hath served in the Army for the space of _Six_ Years and _163_ Days, after the Age of Eighteen, according to the subjoined

STATEMENT OF SERVICE.

IN WHAT CORPS.	PERIOD OF SERVICE.		Serjeant Major.		Qr. Mast. Serjeant.		Serjeant.		Corporal.		Trumpeter or Drummer.		Private.		Service prior to the Age of Eighteen to be deducted.		Total Service.		In Peace or War India, Implied in the storming any Town.	
	From	To	Yrs.	Days	Yrs.	Days	Yrs.	Days	Yrs.	Days	Yrs.	Days	Yrs.	Days	Yrs.	Days	Yrs.	Days	Yrs.	Days
33d Foot	5th June 1812	14th Novr 1810	,,	,,	,,	,,	,,	,,	,,	,,	,,	,,	6	163	,,	,,	6	163	,,	,,
	TOTAL..		,,	,,	,,	,,	,,	,,	,,	,,	,,	,,	6	163	,,	,,	6	163	,,	,,

3rd.
Certificate of the Cause of Discharge.
THAT in consequence of _a Reduction_

HE IS HEREBY DISCHARGED.

4th.
Certificate of not being disqualified for Pension.
THAT he is not to my knowledge, incapacitated by the Sentence of a General Court Martial, from receiving Pension.

5th.
Certificate of Character, &c. &c. &c.
THAT his General Conduct as a Soldier has been _Good_

6th.
Certificate of the Settlement of all Demands.
THAT he has received all just Demands of Pay, Clothing, &c. from his Entry into the Service to the date of this Discharge, as appears by his Receipt underneath.

7th.
Acknowledgment of the Receipt of all Demands.
I _James Robinson_ do hereby acknowledge that I have received all my Clothing, Pay, Arrears of Pay, and all just Demands whatsoever, from the time of my Entry into the Service to the date of this Discharge.

Witnessed by _Jno Longden Capt._

Signature of the Soldier. _James X Robinson_ _his mark_

8th.
Certificate of Description.
TO prevent any improper use being made of this Discharge, by its falling into other Hands, the following is a Description of the said _James Robinson_ He is about _Twenty four_ Years of Age, is _five_ Feet _four_ Inches in height, _brown_ Hair, _Grey_ Eyes, _Sallow_ Complexion, and by Trade or Occupation a _Mason_

my Hand, and the Seal of the Regiment at _Nottingham_ this _14th_ Day of _Novr_ 1818.

Signature of the Commanding Officer. _WH Elphinstone Lt Col 33 Regt_

Guards _14th Novr_ 1810 , confirmed _Jno Macdonald Genl_

An unlikely hero

My story is based on the life of Private James Stokes (1915–45), who hailed from the tenement slums of Glasgow. He became an unorthodox and unlikely hero by winning the Victoria Cross in the Second World War.

Daily Record, *18 April 1945*

It is a love-torn story, starting in the Gorbals. Before D-Day 1944, my great uncle James Stokes was finally settling down with a young family. He had just signed up for the King's shilling when a local thug made clear his intentions towards James's wife. A dance-hall fight broke out, which left the thug in a hospital bed and James in prison. James was sentenced to three years' hard labour for grievous bodily harm, and the powers that reigned during war-time Britain offered him a reprieve and arranged his immediate release to the Army. He went straight into the front line, joining the King's Shropshire Light Infantry.

On the route from Normandy to the small town of Kervenheim, Germany, Jimmy waged war with Rommell's Panzer divisions through the war-torn carnage of western Europe. He single-handedly captured 17 German soldiers, and he was shot eight times. The Victoria Cross, the highest honour bestowed on a British soldier, was awarded posthumously. His wife and small son received the medal but lost a husband, a father and the man they loved.

This is a true story of valour and a journey of the spirit. From the brawling, rubble-strewn, slum backyards to the colossal struggle against Hitler's legions, it is an epic saga of one man's redemption and the freedom won for us.

Anthony Ford

He could not come home

A tall man, impeccably dressed, with bold craggy features sits in an armchair placed by the window. His medals span his left breast from shoulder to lapel. There is no mistaking an Old Soldier, a Tommy – and Ernie, my grandfather, was the last in Ypres.

Ernie looks out upon the flat green landscape stretching to the horizon in every direction broken only by the occasional copse of trees and low hill. Ernie knows these unremarkable features as 'Hill 60' and 'Ypres Salient' and the battles he fought there have lived with him ever since.

Ernie Bennett (1895–1978),
taken a year before he died

Ernie arrived in Ypres in May 1915. In the battle that followed he went over the top four times. The horror of the conditions he and his comrades endured is unimaginable to us today. As he said, 'We were facing towards Hill 60, up to our knees in water much of the time. But if you've not been there it's impossible to imagine, my boy. Impossible.'

Nearly half a million Tommies never returned home.

And neither did my grandfather. He could not. He made Ypres his home and worked for the Commonwealth War Graves Commission, tending the vast cemeteries and memorials to his comrades, except that Ernie called them his mates.

'400,000 of my mates are lying out here,' he said, 'and I'm going to lie next to them.'

And he got his wish when he died on 22 May 1978 and was laid to rest with full military honours at Ypres town cemetery.

Anne Evans

A remarkable record

My grandmother, Lydia Matilda Hurle, was born 18 June 1882 at Blackfriars in London. Later she became Mrs Lydia Upsher when she married my grandfather, Alfred Fearn Upsher. The marriage produced seven children, two boys and five girls. Soon after the marriage she started a family diary, recording all the major events of her family and the nation. One entry reads 'Jan 22nd 1901 Queen Victoria died'.

A typical page from Lydia Upsher's diary

The family in 1952
    Hilda Upsher   *Alfred Upsher*   *Myself* *Lydia Upsher*   *Alfred Upsher*
    (my mother)   *(my grandfather)*   *(my grandmother)* *(my father)*

At the beginning of the Second World War, the Upshers were living in Bantry Street, Camberwell, South London. As for most houses in London, the Government provided a dug-out Anderson shelter situated in the rear garden. It was on the inside of the shelter door that my grandmother started to record, with chalk, all of the German air raids over South London, each entry giving the time the air raid started and the time of the 'all clear'. It wasn't long before the door was full of details and so she transferred everything to a notebook. Interspersed with the dates and times are various details of the types of bombs and anti-aircraft shelling, together with the damage, injuries and deaths in the locality. From the outbreak of war on 3 September 1939 to the final air raid on 28 March 1945, she recorded 1,224 days with 1,198 air raid warnings – a truly remarkable record. I have a copy of her diary and there is also a copy in the Imperial War Museum, London.

Derek Upsher

Victoria Cross

My great-great-grandfather, Robert Kells, was born in India and joined the army aged 13. In 1857, while serving in the 9th Lancers during the Indian Mutiny, he was involved in the siege at Lucknow. He and his captain, Captain Driscoll, were surrounded by the enemy after Driscoll fell off his horse and broke his collar-bone. Robert Kells fought off the enemy and managed to get himself and his captain to safety.

For this action he was awarded the Victoria Cross. He left the army as a trumpet major and came to England for the first time. He worked as a musician and was also a yeoman of the guard at St James's Palace. He died in 1903, aged 74, and is buried in an unmarked grave in Lambeth. Sadly, all his medals were sold by his family for only a few shillings, due to their extreme poverty. They were sold again a few years ago to a businessman in the Middle East for thousands of pounds.

I began looking into the story of Robert Kells about 15 years ago. I went to the Public Record Office at Kew (now the National Archives) and took out all the discharge papers from his regiment with the intention of spending at least a day trying to find his papers. The first box I opened, right on the top, I saw his name, Robert Kells. I now have three sons and the youngest is called Samuel Frederick Kells Haywood.

Jacqueline Haywood

The Redford women at war

In both a family history magazine and at the Imperial War Museum I found a photo of my mother, Beryl Eugenia Leaney nee Redford (1921–92). The photo was used on a postcard and a Second World War recruiting poster for the Women's Auxiliary Air Force (WAAF), which is headed: 'Serve in the WAAF with the men who fly'.

Mum told me that she had been photographed for the poster at the same time as she was filmed by Pathé News being introduced to Princess Marina. However, mum did not see the poster or newsreel, which was screened in cinemas during the war – this was before television became widely available.

Mum helped defend the UK with only a hydrogen-filled barrage balloon between herself and the low-flying German bombers, whose pilots took pot-shots at the balloons with any leftover ammo on their return flights to Germany.

My aunt Joyce Y. Stewart, nee Redford, also served in the WAAF: she was a Spitfire mechanic. I saw a photo of her on display at the Public Record Office (now the National Archives) in Kew. Aunt Joyce became a GI bride when she married an American soldier, and she is still living in the USA.

At the end of January 2003, I wrote to the Imperial War Museum to ask if they would consider having a monument or statue of a woman who fought for her country erected on the vacant plinth in Trafalgar Square.

Susan-Jane Redford Leaney

Anzac Cottage

My grandfather, Cuthbert John Porter, was born in East Dulwich and emigrated to Western Australia in 1911. On the declaration of war in 1914, he was one of the first to join the Australian Imperial Forces. His war was mercifully short. One of the first of the Australian forces ashore at Gaba Tepe in the Dardanelles, he suffered a gunshot wound on 25 April 1915 and was invalided home, arriving in August 1915.

His arrival coincided with a great outpouring of patriotic fervour, and one of the outcomes of this was the decision to build a monument to the gallant Anzacs at Gallipoli. This monument was named Anzac Cottage and was given to my grandfather and his wife, Annie (who had emigrated from Lichfield, Staffordshire, in 1911) as their family home.

Cuthbert John Porter, 1883–1964

Anzac Cottage in 2004

Anzac Cottage is a unique monument. Built using donations of cash, building materials, labour, furniture, fittings and household goods, the cottage was erected in one day. Beginning at 4.30 a.m., 'at the same hour as the men they desire to honor [sic] made their wonderful attack on Anzac Beach', the house was almost complete by bedtime on that day. It was estimated that approximately 200 workmen, aided by a workforce of women providing hot meals and thousands of supporters, all toiled together in the heat of summer to construct Anzac Cottage.

The story of Anzac Cottage is a tale that was built on pride of country, on selfless acts of bravery and on community support and strength.

Anne Chapple

Diary of the Indian Mutiny

In 1956 I discovered, roughly pasted into a family photo album, a diary in faded handwriting dated 1857; it had belonged to my great-great-aunt, Helena Angelo. Her husband, Lieutenant Frederick Angelo of the Indian Army, had been appointed to Cawnpore a few weeks before. This diary had never been read, as apart from the faintness of the ink, it was interspersed with foreign words, which turned out to be Hindi.

Catherine Cortlandt Angelo – the younger of the two little girls smuggled from Cawnpore in 1857– taken a year before her death in 1949 at the age of 95

I slowly deciphered it. When the Indian Mutiny broke out in Cawnpore, Helena, heavily pregnant, described vividly her escape down the river to Allahabad and eventually to Calcutta through the mutinous country, hidden under rugs with her two little girls, and all the time worried about the fate of Frederick.

She had good reason to worry. He was captured at the fall of the cantonment, which had become untenable – no food, water or ammunition – and they were offered safe conduct by Nana Sahib. Instead they were shot down in the small boats transporting them across river.

Those men that survived were murdered, and the women and children were thrown down a well in Cawnpore and butchered just before the relief column arrived. Helena was the last English woman to escape. Frederick's posthumous son was born soon afterwards.

Anne Harden

Remember the Light Brigade

I lifted my grandfather's First World War medals out of the wooden cigar box to show my daughter and, for the first time, noticed a newspaper clipping underneath. It was about my grandfather's retirement, but, mentioned that *his* grandfather was Troop Sergeant Major William Bentley who, as a sergeant, fought with the 11th Hussars in the Charge of the Light Brigade. He was saved from death by Lieutenant Alexander Roberts Dunn, who subsequently received one of the first Victoria Crosses for his bravery.

Troop Sergeant Major Bentley (1816–91), courtesy of Hussars Museum, Winchester

The newspaper cutting which started my ancestral search

I searched for Bentley's name on the internet and found his grave in York. I contacted the man who made the website. He very kindly sent me a page from Lummis and Wynn's book, *Honour the Light Brigade*, giving William's details. From that I decided to try to find out why a farmer's son from Yorkshire ended up in Wiltshire but was buried in York with full military honours! I have a transcript of his funeral. It was very grand so he must have been quite 'high up and respected'.

I have just finished reading a book about George Loy Smith to give me some insight into William's travels. Last week a member of my family sent me the ultimate – a photograph of William! So I have a few 'bits and pieces' but haven't a clue where to start. I know he married twice, which complicates things. I would love to get something together as 2004 is the 150th anniversary of the charge and I think it would be a fitting remembrance.

Margaret Smith

A tingling down my spine

I entered the chapel dedicated to the King's Own Yorkshire Light Infantry and approached the glass case in which lay a large open book. I felt a tingling down my spine. The book contained the names of the men who had been killed in the First World War and staring at me on the open page was the name of my grandfather, Alfred Clough, and the date of his death on 9 January 1915.

Alfred Clough's grave in Bailleuil, France

I later learned that the pages were turned every day. I was flabbergasted. I had woken up that morning with an urge to go to York and visit the Minster. I had never been there before and had no idea the commemorative chapel existed.

The experience took me on a journey of discovery. Thanks to the British Legion, the Commonwealth War Graves Commission, the Ministry of Defence and author Lyn Macdonald, I eventually found my grandfather's grave, while at the same time learning some of the family history.

Patricia Wood

Great Connections

Whether they admit it or not, most family historians live in hope that they can make a connection within their family tree with someone famous or well connected, and thus have a story they can dine out on for years to come. The following contributors have done exactly that. Of course, many families have tall stories about amazing ancestors that have been passed down from generation to generation with only a small grain of truth (if any!) behind the legend. In these instances, diligent research is required to verify the story, and this is the challenge that has been overcome in this collection.

Rubbing shoulders with the great and good of history seems to be a common theme here. There is the story of a young girl who became friends with Napoleon during his exile to St Helena. Another girl was employed as a maid in Queen Victoria's household. Sport features prominently in this section: there is a lovely anecdote about the umpire who incurred the wrath of W. G. Grace by saying he would give him out leg before wicket – apparently 'not the done thing'!

Charles Dickens also makes an appearance via a personal assistant who had some revealing insights into the great author's life. Other featured ancestors who have appeared in literary and entertainment circles include Lord Byron's gondolier, the man who gave the English language the phrase 'Jingoism' and an interpreter for Buffalo Bill's Wild West Show.

Each story provides a glimpse into the everyday lives of prominent figures that we think we know about, yet are told from the perspective of the 'everyday' people who surrounded them. Of course, it helps if you have Lady Luck on your side, as illustrated by the astonishing connections which were revealed during a casual conversation in a youth hostel. You never know when your ancestors are going to catch up with you!

Research Tips

It is a little difficult to provide one set of research notes for such a diverse collection of stories, but the following principles apply. If you suspect a connection with someone famous, look for an official biography and turn to the bibliography or source list. This will identify the primary sources from which the book was written. These sources are likely to have been used to focus on the life and times of the subject, but of course many other documents within the collection were probably discarded during the compilation of the book for being 'irrelevant'.

These documents are precisely where you should look for clues about your ancestors, who are perhaps less likely to feature in 'key' sources used in the book. Of particular use will be personal diaries, journals, and collections of correspondence. However, some private archives may be difficult to gain access to, or require official permission before you can look at items. This can be quite frustrating – but imagine how you would feel if a stranger knocked on your door and asked to look through your personal papers!

Anecdotes about events can at least be placed in a historical context through diligent research in newspapers, published either locally or nationally. Most county archives have a good selection of local papers, while the British Library holds an excellent collection at Colindale in London.

What the Dickens?

I made an extraordinary connection to Dickens when researching my
family tree. My great-great-grandfather's sister, Hannah Manton,
married John Thompson, of Tavistock House, Bloomsbury, in 1852. His
profession? Author's clerk. The author turned out to be Charles
Dickens, whose letters and anecdotes helped reconstruct my ancestor's
life in a way not otherwise possible.

*Tavistock House, where
Charles Dickens lived
1851–9*

*A sketch by Thackeray of
Dickens and friends on
holiday in Cornwall in
1843. John Thompson is
driving the carriage*

St Pancras New Church, Marylebone Road, London, where John Thompson married Hannah Manton in 1852

Thompson, hired by Dickens as his coachman at age 14, was described by the author as 'an excellent servant and a most ingenious fellow', and later as 'a person of Sam Wellerion tendencies and flights'. He acted as Dickens' coachman, clerk and dresser from 1850 onwards, accompanying him on his travels and contributing to his reforming magazine, *Household Words*.

Thompson christened one of his daughters Matilda Dorrit in 1857, after 'Little Dorrit', and literally lived over the shop, in two small rooms over the *Household Words* office. My relative, Hannah Manton, has a small place in history as a result. Evidently she was partial to the strong gin of Victorian days, and Dickens banned her and her sister from the offices! John Thompson played a critical role in Dickens' liaison with the young actress, Ellen Ternan, the subject of Claire Tomalin's 1990 book, *The Invisible Woman*.

In 1866, a theft of eight gold sovereigns from the office was blamed on Thompson. Dickens sought to hush up the whole business and set him up in a small concern. With this Thompson exits from history – as discreet as ever!

Nicholas Waloff

Treading the boards

Philemon Galindo, my great-great-grandfather, was an actor in Bristol during the closing years of the eighteenth century. Descended from Sephardic Jews the family lived in fashionable Clifton not far from Bristol's Theatre Royal where Philemon trod the boards. Playbills in the family possession show him in a variety of roles.

He was a reserve soldier with the Bristol Military Association; perhaps it was the uniform that made him a favourite with the ladies. He married three times. His first wife, the wealthy daughter of a Jamaican sugar plantation owner, gave him two daughters. In Dublin his second wife bore him three children including a handsome son, portrayed in a miniature painting which still exists.

Philemon had a well-documented affair with the actress Sarah Siddons from whom he gained a considerable sum of money. Using this

Philemon Galindo and Mrs Siddons (from The Dublin Satirtis)

A PALPABLE HIT !!!

Catherine Galindo (nee Gough), Philemon's second wife (National Library of Ireland)

The 'handsome son' – a miniature of John Galindo, Philemon's first son by Catherine Gough. He took the name Juan and is shown here in a Colonel's uniform of the army of the Central American Federation

and his wife's capital Philemon became part owner of the Manchester Theatre Royal, a venture that failed miserably. His wife published a series of her letters to Sarah Siddons castigating the affair.

As an army captain in charge of French prisoners in Alton, Hampshire, during the Napoleonic War, he met Anne Jeacock. I am descended from their union. His second wife was still alive.

In 1836 Philemon was appointed to govern a new colony in Bocatoro (now part of Panama). He was accompanied by his son Philip, aged 14, who wrote a journal, still in my possession, about their trip across the Atlantic. The mission was thwarted by the Colombians, leaving them to return home penniless.

John Chappell

Descendant of the Drakes

By far the poorest of all my great-grandparents was Richard Hammett, eventually a paver in Devonport dockyard. His mother, Anne Creber, was the daughter of Henry, a prosperous farmer in Walkhampton, Devon, and his wife Honour Crymes, daughter of Amos, the vicar of Buckland Monachorum from 1752 to 1783. From the late sixteenth century the Crymes, together with the Drakes, had been among the most important families in the area.

When Anne Creber ran away with one of her father's hired hands, Richard Hammett, her family disowned her and, when Anne died and Richard disappeared, let all the children be cared for by Walkhampton parish. Fortunately their son and my great-grandfather – also Richard Hammett – was lucky enough to be placed as apprentice with a kind farmer who treated him well.

Subsequent generations: family photograph taken just after Richard Hammett's funeral in 1862, showing my grandmother Louisa (left), her sister Bessie, and Richard's brother William

My mother, Alma Huxham, and grandmother, Louisa Hammett, 1902

I know this because, although Richard died young, my grandmother was told the story by her mother, and she told my mother. Since then I have been able to trace many of the records which go back to my nine-times-great-grandfather, Thomas Drake. As the youngest brother of Sir Francis Drake, who died childless, Thomas inherited his estate at Buckland Abbey. Thomas shared many of Francis's exploits, including his voyage round the world 1577–80.

Because of the fame of the Drakes my eight-times-great-grandfather, also Sir Francis, was able to make an advantageous marriage into a family which, through Elizabeth Seymour, sister of Henry VIII's third wife Jane, takes my line back to Edward III.

Margaret Filsell

Bear Thunder

My name is Chuck Renuhausay, and I am a full-blood Choctaw/Lakota Sioux native American, now living in London.

My great-grandfather was called Mato Wakinyan (Bear Thunder) and was an interpreter with the Buffalo Bill Wild West Show in the late 1890s when the show toured Great Britain, France and Germany.

Amongst the Sioux, my great-grandpa was a 'whichasha wakan' or holy man who healed many people with his knowledge of ceremonies, plants and herbs. He was both a Yuipi and Heyoka, a medicine man who heals through comical things. We think he joined the Wild West Show to further his knowledge of the 'wasichus' (Europeans) and spent three years here in England.

Images from Buffalo Bill's Wild West show c. 1904. It is likely that one of the native Americans on horseback is my great-grandfather Mato Wakinyan.

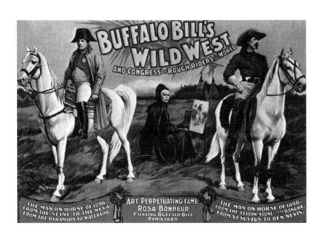

Now I, his great-grandson, am also here, working in a similar tradition as a stand-up comic.

Grandpa always said things went in a circle, and I think this is part of it.

Mitakuye oyasin (all my relations).

Chuck Renuhausay (Bear Thunder)

A frontier-striding preacher

William Carpenter Bompas was born in London in 1834. He was a shy, unsporty, solitary boy in contrast to his father, Charles, on whom Dickens based 'Buzfuz' in *Pickwick Papers*. William's health declined while he worked as a solicitor and he decided to enter the ministry. He was devastated when his first cousin, Selina Cox, rejected his marriage offer.

Discarding his personal possessions, William volunteered for missionary work in Yukon and became an itinerant preacher, in close contact with Eskimos, whose languages he learned in order to spread the gospel.

In 1873 the Diocese of Athabasca was created and Bompas became its first Bishop. When he returned to London for his consecration, Selina finally agreed to marry him. He was 40; she was 44, and a gifted linguist and musician.

Bishop William Carpenter Bompas

The bishop's wife, Selina

Bishop Bompas's simple grave in Carcross, the Yukon

It was a dramatic change of life for her, helping Bompas run a diocese of a million square miles. They ran a school, took in children, and Selina was left for months as he trekked the vast wilderness to 'tend his flock'. During the Gold Rush he witnessed abuses through alcohol and prostitution caused by incoming miners. To protect the indigenous people, he helped establish mounted police posts in the Klondike – the police presence also protected Canadian sovereignty.

Bompas was among the last of the solitary frontier-striding preachers, devoted to Christian preaching, though many misunderstood his preoccupation with indigenous people. He died in June 1906 and was mourned not only by his beloved Selina, but by the people of the Yukon, whether they were Christians or not. He is buried at Carcross. Selina outlived him by ten years.

John Bompas

Life as Queen Victoria's maid

As a child, I heard a family conversation about some letters written by Mariah Baker, my grandfather's great-aunt, and how interesting they might, one day, be to someone. That someone is me!

I am researching the fascinating accounts of my three-times-great-aunt's employment in service as a maid in Queen Victoria's household. Mariah's letters are written from Royal residences throughout Europe, and include letters written on the headed notepaper of Windsor Castle, Balmoral, Dover Castle and St James Palace. Some are written on black-edged writing paper following the death of a member of the royal family.

I am following my ancestor's wonderful insight into royal daily life; her letters are filled with anecdotes of life as a Victorian maid. She writes an account of the death of one of the princes and of her final conversation with him. Mariah's letters include references to Queen Victoria's children and to John Brown, and also a sketch of Queen Victoria at Balmoral.

My preliminary research concludes that Mariah Baker was a maid from c. 1885–8. By 1901 she had returned to her home town of Othery in Somerset and married a dairy farmer. Although settling into a quieter life, I'm sure she had wonderful stories to tell her family through years to come!

Jennie Summerhayes

Pages of letters from Mariah Baker to her sister Nell (Ellen) from Balmoral. One describes a sports day for the royal servants, including an obstacle race and an animal race, which were observed by Queen Victoria from her chair. Afterwards, there was dancing and 'Scotch', with a prize given to the best dancers. Mariah says that 'I shall be very sorry to go from here as I've had such a jolly time'. The letter also refers to John Brown: 'Old John has a lovely tombstone in the churchyard here'. The other concludes with Mariah's sketch of the queen taking exercise.

The fall of Sebastopol

My three-times-great-uncle David was the first station-master at Banchory, Scotland. In September 1855 it was he who took the news of the fall of Sebastopol to Queen Victoria at Balmoral, arriving by horse at about 10.30 p.m.

Cabinet Portrait

GRAY BROTHERS   GATESHEAD ON TYNE

David Middleton, 1825–95

Queen Victoria then told the entire household to turn out and light the bonfire which had been prepared for this news since the previous autumn on Craig Gowan, the hill to the south of the palace. A party was held with the national anthem sung on the top of the hill, watched by Queen Victoria.

Victoria then asked him to ride to Aboyne Castle and tell the Marquis of Huntly, without hesitation and regardless of the hour. He later received a letter from the Queen thanking him for his efforts.

A poem was written commemorating his activity that night:

> A horseman sweeps at the dead of night
> Through the Forest Braes of Mar
> And headlong is his starlit flight
> The messenger of war
> Wildly panteth his foaming steed
> Yet for brae nor bank stays he
> But flies with a highland eagle's speed
> By the rushing waves of Dee.

Fortunately, this was all recorded in his obituary, published in the *Aberdeen Press and Journal* in July 1895, after he died in Camberwell, London.

This corrected the story that had been passed down through the family that he was stationed at Aboyne and carried the news of the relief of Mafeking!

Robin Middleton

Byron's gondolier

My three-times-great-grandfather was Tita Falcieri, Lord Byron's gondolier in Venice. He met many of Byron's friends (including Mary and Percy Shelley, Leigh Hunt and Count D'Orsay). He was with Byron when he died and accompanied the body back to England.

Later Tita went overseas with Lord Clay, and in Malta met Benjamin Disraeli. Clay and Disraeli, later Prime Minister of England, travelled together, with Tita as their valet.

Tita Falcieri (1798–1874),
painted by the artist Daniel
Maclise in 1836
(© The National Trust)

By 1832 Tita was back in England without a job and asked Disraeli for work. Disraeli sent him to be valet to his father in Buckinghamshire. Tita remained there for 19 years serving Isaac D'Israeli, who was himself a famous author. When Isaac D'Israeli died, Tita worked for the India Office in London. He married his co-worker from the Disraeli house and when Tita died Disraeli persuaded Queen Victoria to give his widow a pension.

I have been researching my family tree for ten years and have amassed lots of information. I am writing Tita's biography and have appeared twice on television connected with this. I presented on *50 Places to See Before You Die* on the BBC in 2002, and *The Antiques Ghostshow* on Living TV in 2003.

Tita was an extraordinary character and my aim is to make a documentary about him. His is an amazing tale full of power, intrigue, battles, banishment and famous romantic poets and authors, and yet very few people know about this silent hero.

Claudia Aliffe

Fake royal warrant

Alexander Mackenzie was born in Dunblane, Scotland, and his claim to fame is that in 1842 in Dunblane he shod a carriage horse of Queen Victoria while she was en route from Scotland to London. There may have been some bribing of the queen's coachman involved.

After this, he mounted a fake royal warrant on the corner of his smithy, consisting of a couple of horseshoes and some nails and a crown. There is also a plaque on the wall:

Historic Dunblane
Fake royal warrant

On the corner of this building can be seen the remains of a horse-shoe, nails and crown, placed here by Mr Mckenzie, Blacksmith, after he had re-shoed a horse drawing Queen Victoria's carriage during her visit on 13th September 1842.

Mackenzie died in 1854 following an accident at the smithy in which he was run over by a bolting horse and cart. There is a report of the accident in the *Stirling Observer*.

Duncan Mackenzie

Napoleon's young friend

My father's mother was a Balcombe, descended from the family who lived on the island of St Helena at the time of Napoleon's exile.

Betsy Balcombe was born in 1802, the daughter of a prosperous merchant who was given the job of attending to Napoleon and his officers when Napoleon was sent to live on St Helena.

Napoleon arrived in October 1815. At first Betsy was very frightened because he had always been spoken about as some sort of monster. Until his house was ready, the Balcombe family arranged for him to stay at their house.

Betsy was the only one in her family who could speak French well so Napoleon took to her straight away. She found he was very kind and enjoyed playing games and practical jokes. They often played cards and she taught him Blind Man's Buff.

Napoleon was free to ride and walk on the island and often took Betsy with him. He had his own servants, including a doctor and a chef who made special sweets for Betsy.

Not long after Napoleon moved to his own house, Betsy's mother was taken ill and the family had to sail back to England. Napoleon was sorry see them go and gave Betsy a lock of his hair.

The family never returned to the island and Napoleon died in May 1821.

Rowan Gaydon

Who said family history is dull?

While I was staying in a youth hostel in Buckinghamshire, I got talking to a youngish couple. I asked the lady, who had a foreign accent, where she was from. 'Hertfordshire' was the unexpected answer. I mentioned that my forebears came from there, and something made me go on to say that I was researching my family history and was currently researching a John Watson, who had married Ruth Joiner.

The man showed me an address label which read, 'Barry Watson, Hemel Hempstead'.

'So you are a Watson too?' I asked.

His reply bowled me over: 'This John Watson who married Ruth Joiner, was the wedding at St George's Hanover Square?'

I nearly yelled, 'In 1838, yes, but how on earth would you know that?'

'Because they were my great-great-grandparents,' said Barry.

'But they were mine too!' I shouted.

I then had a creepy feeling we were being watched from another world. Together we established that I was descended from John and Ruth's daughter, while Barry was descended from their son. The family lived in the village of Barkway. We compared notes after that and he gave me the benefit of his research back to the seventeenth century.

He also told me he had an aunt living near my home who had been a Watson before her marriage. When I went to see her, imagine my delight when she produced a wedding photograph which included two great-aunts of mine.

Who said family history is dull? Coincidences like this are rare but can happen to any of us. Here's hoping they happen to you!

Phyllis Jackson

Chariots of Fire

The film *Chariots of Fire* sparked my interest in my family history. One of the characters – Sam Mussabini, the coach – was my great-grandfather.

Scipio Godolphin Mussabini, known as Sam, had cosmopolitan origins as his name might suggest. He was born to Neocles Gaspard Mussabini and Aline Farcat in 1867. Neocles was naturalised as British at the age of 21, but his ancestors came from Damascus. His father was Oriental interpreter to Queen Victoria, reputedly speaking 27 languages. Neocles himself became a journalist and war reporter.

Sam also became a reporter, eventually specialising in athletics and billiards. This led to his involvement in coaching some of the British medallists in the Paris Olympics of 1924, as depicted in *Chariots of Fire*.

The film indicates that Sam was 'persona non grata' at the Olympic stadium because of his professional coaching status, but the truth is more complex.

Early in his career Sam worked on the *Pall Mall Gazette*. Bramwell Booth, of the Salvation Army, approached the editor, W. T. Stead, to expose child trafficking. Sam, writing under the name of Sampson Jacques, was enlisted in the plot to buy a young girl in order to provide the evidence to back up the newspaper story. It was a Victorian sensation and, for his part in it, Sam was sentenced to one month's imprisonment. The Government was then compelled by public pressure to change the law.

This low point in Sam's life is well documented, as is the Olympic highpoint, but the link between the two events is less well known.

Emily Weston

'I shall give you out'

My great-grandfather, Alfred Wallace, was a professional cricketer for ten years and played for Surrey. Later he was called upon to umpire, and it was during a match against Kent that he encountered the great Victorian cricketing legend, W. G. Grace.

Before the match W. G. Grace came up to Alfred and said 'Patsy,' (his cricketing name, so called because of his Irish origin) 'I am *never* out L. B. W.'

The source of the story: my uncle Stan (pictured with auntie Mabel), and his letter which related the encounter between Alfred Wallace (his father) and W. G. Grace

Alfred's response to the great man was, 'Well, sir, if your leg is in front of the stumps when the ball hits it, I shall give you out.'

W. G. was not amused by this answer because at lunch time he bought every player and the other umpire a drink – except Alfred!

Alfred's granddaughter was named Patricia after his cricketing name, and a bale signed by W. G. was handed down in the family. Alfred later opened his own plumbing business in Croydon where Patricia, my cousin, and my own brother still live.

David Hodgson

London's Prime Minister

My grandfather, Isaac Hayward, was born in 1884, in a two-bedroomed terraced house in the mining town of Blaenavon, south Wales. With his brothers and sisters, he received a basic education, but at 12 he was 'adult enough' to start work. His mother obtained the Factory Act Certificate so that he could legally start work in the local mine, Big Pit (now a World Heritage site). Every night, he and his brothers and sisters educated themselves using books from the lending library at the Workman's Hall.

At 16 he joined the union and, through this and the Labour Party, he immersed himself in political activity to improve the lot of others. At the request of two close friends, Ernest Bevin and Herbert Morrison, he moved to London in 1924 where he continued his reforming work, eventually becoming General Secretary of the Enginemen, Firemen and Mechanics Union in 1938.

Sir Isaac Hayward in his office at County Hall shortly after his appointment as Leader of the London County Council

Tribute to Sir Isaac

A ONE-TIME apprentice fitter who left Bleanavon to become 'Prime Minister of London' was this week honoured by his home town — 12 years after his death.

Sir Isaac Hayward — Ike to his friends — was leader of the old London County Council from 1946 to 1964, the highest local authority position in the UK at that time.

During the crucial years of recovering from the effects of the second world war he was second only to the prime minister in terms of administrative power.

On Wednesday of this week Blaenavon Town Council unveiled a plaque commemorating Sir Isaac's birthplace — 13 King Street.

He left for London in the 1920's after becoming prominent in the trade union movement. He had married Alice Mayers, the daughter of a Blaenavon builder, and she and their four sons moved to the Capital with him.

He was a great believer in bringing art to the people and the LCC named the Hayward Gallery after him in recognition of his work in bringing the Festival Hall to the South Bank.

But he was also concerned for the care of people and was largely instrumental in ridding London of the poor-house or workhouse system and bringing in a new era of care for the homeless and the old.

He was knighted in 1959 but, despite all his fame, he never forgot Blaenavon and came home as often as he could. He died in 1976, aged 91.

The Western Mail *report of the 1988 unveiling of the plaque in Blaenavon in Sir Isaac's honour, 12 years after his death*

The application for the birth certificate proving that at 12 years old, Isaac was old enough to work

He was also elected on to the London County Council, became Leader in 1947 and served until 1964 (the longest serving Leader). He was responsible for rebuilding London after the Blitz, with the new homes, schools and hospitals that he believed ordinary people deserved. He was also a major player in the 1951 Festival of Britain and the formation of the South Bank Arts Centre. The press called him 'London's Prime Minister'.

He was knighted in 1959, and in 1968 the Hayward Gallery on the South Bank was named after him. He retired at 80 in 1964 and died in 1976. Sir Isaac Hayward ... quite a transformation for a boy who went to work down a mine when he was 12!

Carole Powell

By Jingo!

I retired in 1992 with two ambitions: to play golf (I have played only once) and research my family history.

My main interest was to find out more about my great-grandfather. My father had shown me a clipping from the *Daily Mirror* 'Old Codgers' who used to answer questions sent in to them. Their reply to a question about the origin of the word 'Jingoism' was that it came from a song sung in the music halls by a chap calling himself 'The Great Macdermott' in 1878.

'That,' said my father 'is your great-grandfather.'

He knew little else, and unfortunately died before I could tell him more. I now have an enormous obituary from the *Daily Telegraph* of 9 May 1901, the day after he died, with a smaller one from *The Times* and another in the theatrical journal *The Era*. He is also mentioned in nearly all the books written

Gilbert Hastings Macdermott,
1845–1901

Extract from obituary in the Daily Telegraph, *9 May 1901*

about the Victorian music hall and is in the 1901 *Who's Who*. With the help of Roy Hudd, I was able to trace his grave in the Norwood cemetery.

He made a small fortune with the 'Jingo Song', which he bought from a man named Hunt for a few shillings. He sang other songs of the time, like 'Champagne Charlie', and wrote plays. After going bankrupt in 1885, he came back to manage several music halls and become an agent. His daughter's wedding in 1909 was attended by Marie Lloyd. His real name was John Farrell and his father was an Irish bricklayer, over here to escape the famine, I would imagine.

Brian Farrell

The father of public health in India

Although our family tree starts in 1708 my story is about the achievements of my great-grandparents.

Colonel Walter Gawen King,
1851–1935

> 'Such was his vital force and so sound and true were his ideas that despite difficulties he won through ... India owes Walter Gawen King a debt which it can never repay.'

Extract from Walter's obituary in The Lancet, *13 April 1935*

In April 1935 *The Lancet* described my great-grandfather, Colonel Walter Gawen King, as 'the father of public health in India'. The King's Institute of Preventative Medicine, Madras, was named after him and still exists.

After graduating from Aberdeen University in 1873, he entered the Indian Medical Service and, after holding important posts in Madras, including two professorships, he was appointed sanitary commissioner to the government of Madras and later of Burma. He received special thanks for his work during the famines of 1876–7 and 1896–7 and the accompanying cholera epidemics. In 1899 he was awarded the CIE (Companion of the Indian Empire).

He upset previous ideas that sanitation was a fad. He was determined to do something for people in his care; the control of smallpox, cholera and other diseases was of paramount importance for him.

It was no desk job and his duties took him into the villages, touring the Irrawaddy by boat with my great-grandmother, Laura. He was a brave man and often risked his life to shoot marauding tigers which had killed people in the villages he inspected.

In spite of nine children, and several from a previous marriage, Laura found time to paint the flora of Burma and Madras. On her death in 1918, 15 albums containing 1,017 paintings were presented to the Royal Botanic Gardens in Kew, where they remain useful for reference.

Stephanie Hellewell

Taking It Further

Useful addresses

College of Arms
Queen Victoria Street
London EC4V 4BT
www.college-of-arms.gov.uk

Family Records Centre
1 Myddelton Street
London EC1R 1UW
020 8392 5300
0870 243 7788 (for birth, marriage and death certificate enquiries)
www.familyrecords.gov.uk/frc

Federation of Family History Societies
PO Box 2425
Coventry CV5 6YX
www.ffhs.org.uk

The Genealogical Society of Utah
British Isles Family History Service Centre
185 Penns Lane
Sutton Coldfield
West Midlands B76 8JU
www.lds.org.uk/genealogy/fhc

General Register Office for Scotland
New Register House
Edinburgh EH1 3YT
0131 313 4433
www.gro-scotland.gov.uk

Guild of One-Name Studies
c/o Society of Genealogists
Website: www.one-name.org.uk

Institute of Heraldic and Genealogical Studies
79–82 Northgate
Canterbury CT1 1BA
01227 768664
www.ihgs.ac.uk

National Archives of Ireland
Bishop Street
Dublin 8
Ireland
00 3531 407 2300
www.nationalarchives.ie

National Archives of Scotland
HM General Register House
Princes Street
Edinburgh EH1 3XY
0131 556 6585
www.open.gov.uk/gros/groshome.htm

Public Record Office of Northern Ireland
66 Balmoral Avenue
Belfast BT9 6NY
028 9025 5905
proni.nics.gov.uk

Society of Genealogists
14 Charterhouse Buildings
Goswell Road
London EC1M 7BA
020 7251 8799
www.sog.org.uk

The National Archives
Ruskin Avenue
Kew
Richmond
Surrey TW9 4DU
020 8392 5200
www.nationalarchives.gov.uk

Additional websites
www.1901census.nationalarchives.gov.uk
www.ancestry.co.uk
www.bbc.co.uk/history
www.cyndislist.com
www.documentsonline.nationalarchives.gov.uk
www.familysearch.org
www.freebmd.org.uk
www.genesreunited.co.uk
www.genuki.org.uk
www.movinghere.org.uk
www.nationalarchives.gov.uk/archon
www.rootsweb.com
www.thehistorychannel.co.uk

Software
Family Historian (Calico Pie – see www.family-historian.co.uk)
Family Tree Genealogy Suite (GSP – see www.gsp.cc).
Family Tree Maker (Genealogy.com – see www.genealogy.com)

Books

A. Bevan, *Tracing Your Ancestors in the Public Record Office*, 6th edn (Public Record Office, 2002)

R. Blatchford, *The Family and Local History Handbook* (Robert Blatchford, 2004)

P. Christian, *The Genealogist's Internet* (The National Archives, 2002)

S. Colwell, *The Family Records Centre: A User's Guide* (Public Record Office, 2002)

S. Fowler, *The Joys of Family History* (Public Record Office, 2001)

S. Fowler, *Tracing Your First World War Ancestors* (Countryside Books, 2003)

S. Fowler and W. Spencer, *Army Records for Family Historians* (Public Record Office, 1998)

D. T. Hawkings, *Criminal Ancestors: A Guide to Historical Criminal Records In England and Wales* (Sutton, 1992)

M. D. Herber, *Ancestral Trails* (Sutton, 1997)

D. Hey, *Family Names and Family History* (Hambledon and London, 2000)

D. Hey, *Journeys in Family History: The National Archives' Guide to Exploring Your Past – Finding Your Ancestors* (The National Archives, 2004)

D. Hey, *The Oxford Companion to Local and Family History* (Oxford University Press, 1996)

E. C. Joslin, A. R. Litherland and B. T. Simpkin, *British Battles and Medals* (Spink, 1988)

R. Kershaw, *Emigrants and Expats* (Public Record Office, 2002)

R. Kershaw and M. Pearsall, *Immigrants and Aliens*, 2nd edn (The National Archives, 2004)

S. Lumas, *Making Use of the Census*, 4th edn (Public Record Office, 2002)

E. McLaughlin, *Laying Out a Pedigree* (Federation of Family History Societies, 1990)

The National Archives, *The Family History Starter Pack* (The National Archives, 2004)

B. Pappalardo, *Tracing Your Naval Ancestors* (The National Archives, 2003)

G. Pelling, *Beginning your Family History*, 7th edn (Federation of Family History Societies, 1998)

R. Perks, *Oral History: Talking about the Past* (Historical Association, 1992).

R. Pols, *Family Photographs, 1860–1945* (Public Record Office, 2002)

Reader's Digest, *Explore Your Family's Past: Trace Your Roots and Create a Family Tree* (Reader's Digest, 2002)

P. Saul, *Family Historian's Enquire Within*, 5th edn (Federation of Family History Societies, 1995).

W. Spencer, *Army Service Records of the First World War*, 3rd edn (Public Record Office, 2001)

W. Spencer, *Air Force Records for Family Historians* (Public Record Office, 2000)

I. Swinnerton, *Sources for Family History in the Home* (Federation of Family History Societies, 1995)

J. Titford, *Writing Up Your Family History* (Countryside Books, 2004)

Magazines
All of the following are available monthly from your local newsagent:

Ancestors
The National Archives/Wharncliffe Publishing
– the official family history magazine from TNA, featuring advice from the experts
www.ancestorsmagazine.co.uk/

Family History Monthly
Diamond Publishing
– carrying a range of articles, with a comprehensive online section

Family Tree Magazine
ABM Publishing
– the longest-established magazine, 20 years old in 2004
www.family-tree.co.uk/

Practical Family History
ABM Publishing
– offering basic advice for the novice family historian
www.family-tree.co.uk/

Your Family Tree
Future Publishing
– launched in 2003, and featuring a monthly CD cover mount
www.yourfamilytreemag.co.uk/

Index to Contributors